WITHOUT WARNING

The Great Storm of 1953

CARMEL KING

Ian Henry Publications

Published by
Ian Henry Publications, Ltd.,
20 Park Drive, Romford, Essex RM1 4LH
and printed by
Book*sprint*, New Barn, Milverton, Wellington TA21 0QJ

Acknowledgements

I have had the most life-altering experience while researching for this book. It has made me more aware of the person I am and restored my confidence in people. I have met (and had correspondence) with some of the most wonderful people I have ever had the pleasure of knowing.

I would like to give special thanks to the Manser family, formerly of Canvey Island – Andrew, Graham, Margaret, and Malcolm, who all took the time to talk about the flood, something they had never done all together until Graham saw my press appeal just before the 50th anniversary commemorations. We have kept in contact by post and Andrew took the time to draft a copy of the events as he remembered them, before the others gave their approval and it was passed on to me. I am so very grateful to them, as I realise it was a very delicate matter and that they still miss their three baby brothers.

I would also like to thank the following, who told me their personal recollections of events: Mr Arthur Bensley of Gold Coast, Australia, formerly of Gorleston-on-Sea, Norfolk; Mr George Frost of Canvey Island; Mrs Gwen Rawlingson, the Honorary Parish Archivist for Great Wakering; Mrs Rosalind Boyce of Lincolnshire; Mr James Marshall of Stranraer; Mr Robert Nelson of Stranraer; and Mr Colin W Ash, formerly of the Isle of Sheppey, Kent.

The following people gave me help in my quest for photographs and information: Mrs Shirley Blythe of Ayrshire, who gave me mountains of information and kept me up to date with the 50th anniversary services in Scotland; Andrew Service of Stranraer; Geoff Barsby of Canvey Island; John Lovett of Aldeburgh, Suffolk; Len Whittaker of Ingatestone, Essex; Valerie Stone of Laindon, Essex; and Sarah Ward at the Essex Police Museum.

A big thank you to the following for all their help with this book: Canvey Island Branch Library; Southend-on-Sea Library; Lincolnshire County Library; Norfolk County Library; Essex County Council; Suffolk County Council; Kent County Council; Lincolnshire County Council; Museum of Lincolnshire Life; Essex Record Office in Southend-on-Sea and in Chelmsford; Bexley Archives; Environment Agency; the Meteorological Office; All Books, Mill Road, Maldon; the *Yellow Advertiser*, *Evening Echo* and *Standard Recorder*.

The lovely people of Sea Palling must also be thanked for their kindness in helping me locate the village's flood memorial. To the kind gentleman who gave me and my husband directions to St Margaret's Church, so that we could photograph the beautiful memorial bench he had just finished restoring. And to the people in the café next to the sand dunes who gave me information on the memorial service.

CK

Prologue

Everyone jokes about the 'British weather', but in reality we are usually lucky enough not to suffer at the hands of Mother Nature's wrath when she lets loose killer weather. The British Isles don't suffer devastating earthquakes or terrifying tornadoes. We don't live under the threat of volcanoes or get hit by frequent hurricanes. Generally, the worst we have to suffer is an unexpected downpour in the middle of a summer picnic! But occasionally, and very rarely, we experience freak weather. A winter flurry of snow can sometimes be a Siberian weather system blown off course and we wake to discover our homes have been blocked in by three feet of cold white crispy flakes. Or the tail end of an Atlantic hurricane may drift into another weather system, sending it spinning out of control on to our shores and lashing us with Force 12 gales up to 125 mph. One of these times was the weekend of 31st January – 1st February 1953.

Britain had enjoyed almost a year with a new monarch, Queen Elizabeth II, and was recovering well from World War II. New homes were been built and the economy was beginning to look good. No one in their wildest dreams would have thought we would have been attacked again; only this time by an unseen force that was to push the contents of the North Sea into our homes and businesses while we slept soundly, only to be awoken by the thunderous roar of water breaching the sea wall defences and crashing into our bedrooms. Some would never wake.

The storm was to cost 307 lives and the death of over 46,000 livestock made up of cattle, sheep, pigs, horses, and poultry. Hundreds of miles of road made impassable, alongside over 200 miles of wrecked rail track. The cost was phenomenal, including £50 million in 1953 money to repair and improve the coastal defence system.

This book follows the path of the storm from its birth and as the winds gather speed as it approaches Scotland, sinking numerous fishing vessels and the passenger ferry M.V. *Princess Victoria* causing the deaths of 133 people. The storm then veers around Scotland and heads along the east coast of England causing a devastating tidal surge. Nearly all the coastal towns and villages from East Riding in Yorkshire to Margate in Kent were taken by surprise and practically washed out, as were thousands in the Low Countries.

I have tried to include as many towns and villages as I could, with personal stories that have been told to me and those I have read about. I have also included up to date stories from the 50th Anniversary memorials.

CK

Chapter One

The birth of the storm

Thursday, 29th January, 1953

A slow moving depression is discovered by the Meteorological Office and located between the Azores and Iceland. During the afternoon it is recorded to be travelling northeast, then east-north-east and deepening. By that night it is on course for the coast of Scotland and the pressure at its core is falling.

Friday, 30th January

At 6 am, still descending on Scotland, the pressure at the depression's centre has now fallen below normal. During the afternoon west-north-westerly winds have begun pushing water from the North Atlantic into the North Sea. That night, the depression enters the North Sea veering to the north-west.

Severe gales were now battering the Scottish Isles and off the coast of the Hebrides the Clan Steam Liner *Clan MacQuarrie* is no match for the tempest. After her captain and crew struggle bravely to fight the giant waves and the fierce gales, she runs aground just off the Butt of Lewis.

8.30 pm - Stranraer, Dumfries, Scotland

The fireman for the Dumfries passenger train, 32 year-old James Marshall, went to the assistance of a woman struggling to get off the train with luggage and two very young boys. The woman wanted to board the train from Glasgow, which was waiting on the other platform to take passengers down to the port for the 7 am ferry to Larne in Northern Ireland. . James Marshall picked up the smaller of the two boys and grabbed one of the woman's suitcases. He told her to follow him over the open bridge to the other platform. They all battled in the wind to get across the bridge. Once on the train the woman turned to Mr Marshall to give him something for helping her.

"Don't be daft!" he said, and explained he had young children of his own. Then he said words he would soon be regretting for the rest of his life, "You will be all right when you get on the boat," he told her. He then went back over the bridge to his train.

10 pm – Outer Hebrides, Scotland

Sixteen-year-old George Palin waves goodbye to his mother as he sets off to join the crew of the fishing trawler *Michael Griffith*. His mother was fretting about the terrible weather, but he told her he would be fine and not to worry so much. This would be George's second trip on the trawler; they had returned to port the day before with boiler trouble, but now she was fixed and the crew needed the fish – to pay the wages that put bread on the table! The boat cast off for the fishing grounds off Lewis in what seemed to be a usual winter storm.

Saturday, 31st January

<u>1 am – Outer Hebrides, Scotland</u>
The crew of the *Michael Griffith* were now in severe jeopardy as the 100 mph winds, Gale Force 10, battered the trawler and sent 60 feet waves crashing over the deck. It wasn't long before the crew sent their first S.O.S. signal, saying that the boat was full of sea water and had no steam: they were helpless and asked for a ship to come to their rescue.

<u>6 am - The Orkney Isles, Scotland</u>
The pressure at the depression's centre is now critically low. Coinciding with the spring tides and a full moon, the east coast of Britain was about to experience their horrifying consequences.

Chapter Two

The *Princess Victoria* ferry disaster, wind speed recordings and the loss of the Fleetwood trawler, *Michael Griffith*

<u>7.45 am - Stranraer, Dumfries, Scotland</u>
After a 45-minute delay, Captain James Millar Ferguson begins to sail his passenger ferry, M. V. *Princess Victoria* from Stranraer and heads up Loch Ryan. The sailing had been delayed due to bad weather reports in the North Channel of the Irish Sea, but news had come in that the winds were beginning to die down on the Irish side of the water and the Captain took the decision to resume schedule. All was well as the ferry sailed up the loch; there were 176 men, women, and children on board the 2,694-ton vessel and some motor vehicles on the car decks.

At 9 am, the *Princess Victoria* rounded the head of the loch at Milleur Point and felt the full force of the raging storm. The captain tried to turn the vessel back to Stranraer, but the colossal waves pounded the stern doors until they burst open, flooding the car decks. This caused the vessel to list to starboard and drift out into the North Channel. David Broadfoot, the ship's wireless operator, wasted no time in sending the first distress signal; he sent a Morse code S.O.S. stating their position and asked for the assistance of a tug as the ship was no longer under command. Unknown to the crew of the *Victoria*, no tugs were available; the nearest tug had gone to the assistance of the *Clan MacQuarrie*. David Broadfoot sent another S.O.S. message stating that the crew had been unsuccessful in their attempts to close the stern doors and that the ship was listing badly.

<u>9 am - Stranraer</u>
Geordie McMillan knocked on the door of the railway fireman, James Marshall. He had news that the *Princess Victoria* was in trouble in the loch. Geordie's younger brother, David, worked on the ferry and Geordie and his other brother Jerry worked on the railways with James.

<u>9.30-10.30 am - The Orkney Islands, Scotland</u>
A wind speed of 90 mph with 125 mph gusts was recorded with an average wind speed of Force 11.

<u>10.26 am - Rothesay, Bute, Scotland</u>
The S.O.S. message from the *Princess Victoria* is relayed to Lieutenant Commander H. P. Flemming on the H.M.S *Contest*, the duty destroyer at Rothesay. They are ordered by the Captain of the 3rd Submarine Flotilla to assist in the recovery of the passenger ferry.

<u>11 am - 12 noon - Aberdeenshire, Scotland</u>
An average wind speed of Gale Force 10 is recorded, with 80 mph gusts. Thousands of acres of forest are flattened by the gales. For the forest, wildlife, and the people of Scotland, this is a disaster on a colossal scale.

Princess Victoria officers: Shirley Duckels (Chief Officer), David Broadfoot (wireless operator), James Millar Ferguson (Captain), William McInnes (2nd engineer)

Photograph: Dumfries and Galloway Museums Service

1 pm - The North Channel, Irish Sea
HMS *Contest* reaches the position given by the *Princess Victoria*, but there is no sign of the ferry. The commander decides to continue southwards to search for the ferry.

1.10 pm - Harwich, Essex
Unaware of the tragedy unfolding in the Irish Sea, the members of the Harwich and Dovercourt Sailing Club were going about their usual Saturday afternoon business.

Members dressed for the weather in rubber boots, jumpers, waterproofs and woolly hats, all painting and repairing their boats to take to sea in better weather. The wind was fierce and had an icy bite. Just inside Harwich harbour at Parkeston Quay the locals were holding their ambulance competitions, ignoring the gale force winds that were lashing against the sand dunes and concrete sea defences; life was carrying on as normal.

1, 15 pm - Off the coast of County Down, Northern Ireland

Passengers and crew on the *Princess Victoria* were now using buckets and anything they could lay their hands on to bail out the water that had begun seeping into the lounge area. Captain Ferguson struggled and clambered his way past his passengers that littered the rooms and gangways of the ship. The people were holding on to whatever furniture was bolted to the floor. Children were crying and the walls and floors were spattered in vomit from the last 5 hours enduring a terrifying roller coaster ride. The Captain called for attention and ordered the men to link arms in a chain to help the women and children get to the lifeboats. All the women and children managed to fit snugly into one single lifeboat. As the crewmembers began to lower away a fault developed in the rope mechanism, this was probably due to the terrible conditions. Suddenly, the lifeboat plummeted into the fierce seas and a huge wave scooped up the boat and slammed it into the hull of stricken ferry. Every single woman and child that had been on board the *Princess Victoria* was killed. The crew members and male passengers of the ferry could only watch in horror as the thunderous roar of the waves muffled the spine-tingling screams of the women and children and their bodies vanished from sight.

At 1.35 pm, Captain Ferguson spots the Irish Coast and at 1.45 pm David Broadfoot sends a message giving the ship's position off Belfast Loch. He sends a final message at 1.58 pm to the H.M.S. *Contest*, repeating the position off Belfast Loch.

At 2 pm the M.V. *Princess Victoria* founders, just after Captain Ferguson gives the order to abandon ship. Captain James Millar Ferguson and wireless operator, David Broadfoot, remain at their posts, as the doomed car ferry is dragged to the bottom of the Irish Sea. Two other victims are Sir Walter Smiles, Ulster Unionist Member of Parliament for North Down and J Maynard Sinclair, Deputy Prime Minister and Minister of Finance in the Northern Ireland Assembly.

44 survivors of the *Victoria* are rescued by lifeboats, notably that from Donaghadee, County Down.

2 pm - Outer Hebrides, Scotland

It had become apparent that *Michael Griffith*, the trawler captained by Charles Singelton, was lost. After a long battle with the elements, the sea finally takes her. Her crew of fifteen fine men were dragged down with her, just off Barra Head.

Chapter Three

Flooding in Sutton-on-Sea, Anderby Creek, Chapel St Leonards, Mablethorpe, Hunstanton, Saltfleet, King's Lynn, Sea Palling and the first stages of Great Yarmouth flood

<u>5 pm - Sutton-on-Sea, Lincolnshire</u>

Station Road, Sutton-on-Sea
From Museum of Lincolnshire Life, by courtesy of Lincolnshire County Council, Education and Cultural Services Directorate

At Sandilands, at the southern end of Sutton-on-Sea, the sea crashes in through the already breached dunes. The High Street in Sutton is awash and the water level is rising fast. The sea had smashed inland at Acre Gap and the water had spread four miles past Sutton through a 1,400 feet space laid bare on the beach, dragging thousands of tons of sand with it. The sea defences that used to be where now only a gaping hole was, used to be made up of wooden posts that were piled deep into the sand; the mighty sea ripped the whole lot out. The sea deposits the sand the waves had dragged with them, in piles ranging from 1 foot to 8 feet in height. Every street is blocked and every home choked by the golden grains that poured in like an avalanche.

Two photographs of sand piled at the sides of roads in Sutton-on-Sea after the water had subsided.
*From Museum of Lincolnshire Life, by courtesy of Lincolnshire County Council,
Education and Cultural Services Directorate*

The sand hills at Sandilands were washed inland, smothering thousands of acres of valuable farmland. The residents fled as their homes were torn down. The sea smashed the concrete sea defences that lined the coast and they crumbled into the waves. All the way to Chapel Point another part of the sea wall, made of earth, is washed away, the sea bounces off the inner wall and floods back into Chapel Marsh, swamping the village in 5 feet of icy seawater. The bungalows have their contents ripped out; beds, chairs, tables, and wardrobes join the mounds of swollen dead livestock and debris. They all smash violently against the wall at the lower end of the marsh, aided by the gale force winds. 16 people had been killed.

5.30 pm - Anderby Creek, Lincolnshire
The water had begun to rise rapidly. The force of the water pushes two farm buildings, weighing about 15 tons each, quite a distance. A man was sitting in his home when the water burst through unexpectedly. He ran to the safety of his first floor to await rescue.

6.45 pm - Chapel Point, Lincolnshire
The sea wall, after taking a ferocious beating, finally gives way and overturns, sending water gushing inland.

At nearby Chapel St Leonards, a couple left their house to investigate the crying of their pet dog, to discover their bungalow was surrounded by rapidly rising flood water. They waded through waist deep water to find higher ground while their dog swam alongside them. They found a place to shelter under some bushes, where they spent the night.

7 pm - Canvey Island, Essex
Captain Dennis Brown had opened the new War Memorial Hall earlier that evening, in honour of the 57 islanders who perished in World War II. The party was now in full swing and people chatted light-heartedly about the terrible gales outside and about the awaited opening of the new Benfleet Secondary School, or 'The Palace', as it was nicknamed due to the quality of the new modern building. It was due to open that coming Monday, and many people had baked cakes and biscuits for the grand opening.

Canvey War Memorial Hall

Some people left the War Memorial party and boarded a coach bound for a dance on Southend Pier.

Also on Canvey Island that evening, the Rio Cinema in Furtherwick Road was packed with people watching the Saturday night film, *Beau Geste,* starring Gary Cooper, fighting the Arabs in the desert heat. 10 year-old Andrew Manser, with his 13 and 14 year old brothers, Chris and Ian, left the cinema as the movie finished and headed home along the Winter Gardens path; skipping and jumping cautiously over obstacles in the darkness along the broken concrete path on top of the sea wall. It was very windy, but not as cold as previous nights. The boys recalled how they had played at their bedroom window, just after Christmas, breathing on the glass pane to melt the ice that had formed on it during the cold night; they were sure it was definitely warmer that evening. Ahead the three brothers could see their bungalow that they shared with their parents, five younger brothers, and little sister. Malcolm was 8, Graham 7, and Keith was 5 and had just begun attending the local primary school. Their sister, Margaret, was 4 and the two babies, Gordon and Alan, were just 2 and 1 years of age.

The boys jumped down the concrete steps down off the sea wall path and skipped along the grass track that led to their home. The bungalow was a typical Canvey residence, a holiday chalet that was built on brick pillars; this helped keep the rainwater out whenever it rained heavily. The veranda at the front of the property had a shallow pitched tin roof and was made from and iron frame with glass on the top level and asbestos sheeting along the base. Ian, Chris, and Andrew opened the sliding doors of the veranda and went through the inner door to the lounge, bursting to tell their parents all about the film they had seen.

Soon after, the children were all packed off to bed; Andrew and Malcolm shared a bed in the same room as Chris and Graham, who shared another bed. Their bedroom was situated to the rear of the property and was an extension, built almost at ground level on a concrete base. Margaret slept in her parents' room along with Alan and Gordon who slept in the pram. Ian shared the smaller bedroom with Keith. Andrew fell asleep immediately.

7.10 pm - Mablethorpe, Lincolnshire

The coastguard at the Mablethorpe Coastguard Office was frantically trying to contact the police station. Gigantic waves were smashing the sea wall to pieces and within minutes had burst through, washing 860,000 tons of sand into the little streets.

A man sitting in his lounge watching his wife stoke the fire notices something out of the corner of his eye. He turnes to look out of the back door and sees a strange glimmering; thinking that it was snowing he goes to investigate. As he opens the door a 4 foot wall of water met him and sent him flying across the room; his poor wife was swamped. Somehow they manage to struggle to their feet and get outside. The woman called out for their dog, but her husband dragged her on before the water got too deep. Their pet dog had found safety on the floating dining table.

In the town the residents were scrambling to find higher ground; the strong helped the weak and the young helped the old. A man who had found a sturdy piece of ground to stand on called out to a young mum who was up to her waist in the gushing torrent, trying to hold her baby above the water. She lost her footing and plunged into the icy water; the cruel current snatched her baby from her grasp, leaving her wailing in anguish.

Doors, tables, and chairs danced down the streets like a parade on water. Homes filled with sand and the water flowed in a deafening roar. An old man had to watch helplessly as his disabled wife was dragged to her death.

An off-duty policeman, P.C. Midgeley, ran up to the first floor of his home as the flood poured in and opened his bedroom window that looked down on the street. He could see his elderly neighbours struggling to get out of their flooded bungalow. The flood was deepening rapidly and the current had become dangerously strong. Unable to just stand and do nothing as his neighbours got into difficulties, P.C. Midgeley jumped into the fast flowing water, which was now up to his shoulders, and helped the elderly couple into his house. He then rescued a woman from a tree and a passing newspaper delivery boy, who was still clinging to his pushbike. Eventually seventeen cold, wet, and shocked people filled the bedrooms of his house.

Mablethorpe residents being taken to safety, 2nd February, 1953
From Museum of Lincolnshire Life, by courtesy of Lincolnshire County Council,
Education and Cultural Services Directorate

Just along the coast at nearby Skegness was the Butlin's holiday camp. The sea wall was, knocked flat by the constant battering of the sea sending water rushing inland. The holiday park was swamped in 6 feet of icy cold seawater. 20 people were drowned in the unexpected flood.

Mablethorpe High Street
*From Museum of Lincolnshire Life, by courtesy of Lincolnshire County Council,
Educational and Cultural Services Directorate*

7.27 pm - Hunstanton, Norfolk

Along the coast to Snettisham all the bungalows and beach huts were savaged by the waves; whipped up into frenzy by the powerful storm force winds. Some were just damaged, others totally destroyed, or simply torn from where they stood and deposited in fields or along the railway line that swept along near the seafront.

The 7.27 pm King's Lynn to Hunstanton train was puffing along in the track on its last stop approach to Hunstanton Railway Station. The darkness lit by the headlamp on the front of the steam engine. As the driver prepared to apply the brakes, he found himself slamming them on violently. A wall of water, several feet high, was travelling at great speed towards the screeching train. The driver managed to keep the train from derailing as they hit the speeding wave, but then, something else was coming at them through the darkness; it was one of the bungalows! It hit the train with tremendous force, sending a surge of water pouring into the engines cab and flooding the furnace. This sent steam rocketing out in all directions. The driver and crew were lucky enough to dodge the scalding spray. They had a long night ahead of them, trying to dry out the furnace and relight the fire.

By 7.40 pm, along the coastline at Hunstanton, tucked in snugly behind the sea wall were 40 cosy little bungalows, built on low-lying land. Among the residents huddled up inside their homes were 12 American servicemen and their families. Much to the disgust of some of the locals, who believed the homes that the airmen were renting could have been used for 'local needs'. This made the Americans unpopular and they were made to feel

13

unwelcome by some of the locals. The children were tucked up warm in their beds and the men and women were cuddling up on their sofas. Some were listening to the radio programme that was being broadcast that evening, some were sipping hot drinks and reminiscing about home. Then the sea raged in with no warning whatsoever. Parents ran into the bedrooms to save their children as the angry foaming water chased them, the waves swirling up and around their waists, higher and higher until... it's too late. 65 men women and children were killed along this stretch of the Norfolk coastline. Some of the lucky ones clung to anything they could find above the water level in a fight for survival.

7.45 pm - King's Lynn, Norfolk

Water surges up the Great Ouse River, overflowing into the streets. People were trapped in their homes as the water gushes through their streets. They can only watch helplessly as the river snatches 15 lives as it crashes around every corner and charges down every street like a herd of bulls. Flood warnings flash up on cinema screens and the police tour the streets with loudspeakers, warning the residents. The water swept over the bank at Cut Bridge and poured into the narrow streets surrounded by Queen's Avenue and Wisbech Road. The speeding water then begins to flow on over fields and allotments near Hardwick Road, drowning hundreds of pigs, then on towards South Lynn Railway Station. One and a half thousand people had to be evacuated from the South Lynn Estate.

7.45 pm - Saltfleet, Lincolnshire

A man is standing at his sink, washing the dishes after supper, when he narrowed his eyes to look out of the window into the darkness. To his horror, lit by the moon, he sees a giant wave coming across the sand dunes at great speed. He runs for his life and heads for higher ground. He is one of the lucky ones.

Earlier that day a female resident of Saltfleet had been chatting to her elderly next-door neighbour, telling her to ring her emergency bell if she needed anything; the women had a doorbell system between their houses, so that the 80 year-old woman could get help if she needed it. The younger woman had already climbed the bookcase to escape the rising floodwater, when she first heard the bell ringing. The 80 year-old woman was trapped in her lounge, ringing the bell frantically. The water was too dangerous for the young woman to attempt to get next door, so she had to stay put at the top of her bookcase, listening to the bell getting fainter and fainter, until it eventually stopped. The young woman's head touched the ceiling and she was desperately trying to stop the water going into her mouth; lucky for her it had stopped rising, not so lucky for her elderly neighbour.

Life in other towns was still going on at its usual pace. At Southend-on-Sea the music played and the people danced happily in the Pier Ballroom as the tide crept rapidly up each iron leg of the one and three-quarter mile deck. In Great Yarmouth's Floral Hall, men and women were happily dancing the night away at the weekly dance evening, while the floodwaters lapped menacingly against the concrete steps.

By this time Southend Pier was two feet away from the peak tide level, which wasn't expected until 1.42 am. The pier's duty officer, after seeing this, goes into the pier attendant's office to telephone the coastguard and report in to Southend police station.

8 pm - Sea Palling, Norfolk

In the Nissen hut that was being used as the village hall, the locals were engrossed in a Whist Drive. The door flew open making everyone jump as a gust of wind took it and slammed it against the wall. The vicar stood in the doorway, he appeared to want to say something, but was stuck for words. He removed his hat nervously, as all eyes in the room focused on him. He told them that the sea had broken through the sand dunes and was rising fast. For a moment everyone sat stunned as the wind blew through the hall, whisking up cards and ruffling people's hair. Then the villagers sprung into action. People knocked on doors to warn of the danger and farmers herded their livestock up to higher ground. One farmer, over 6 feet in height, carried a calf on his shoulders as he ran behind his herd of cattle.

As the sea swelled over the dunes, the houses are literally rolled over by the force of the tidal wave as it crashes in. The baker's, café, and general store are all swept away, taking with them a great chunk of the Lifeboat Public House. The landlord of the Lifeboat tried desperately to swim to a rescue boat, but he disappeared beneath the surface before hands could reach him. Two elderly ladies climbed up on to the roof of their bungalow, but one lost her footing and slipped off into the fast moving water. A girl from the village had just finished her paper round and was heading for home when the sea caught up with her and drowned her. Her mother and father had come out of their bungalow to get to safety, the father carrying his baby daughter on his back. The sea snatches her away as they were engulfed by the salt water, they manage to save themselves but have lost their two precious daughters. The flood takes another child and an elderly woman.

Another family are in their home getting supper ready, when there is a knock on the door. It is one of the local farmer's daughters who warned the family of the approaching surge. The mother and daughter remained in the kitchen, while the father and a friend who had come to stay went out to investigate. It was a matter of minutes before the mother and daughter heard their screams and they both ran up the garden path to be met by huge wave that dragged them back into the bungalow. They scrambled back outside for fear of drowning, when their elderly neighbour and her daughter opened the back door. With both doors open the sea swept through the property, dragging the contents with it. The mother wailed as the inside of her home was destroyed in front of her eyes. The five women and the father managed to climb up on to the roof of the bungalow and there they sat, huddled against the chimneystack in the fierce wind.

8 pm - Great Yarmouth, Norfolk

Water from the River Yare had been constantly flooding, slowly but steadily, since 7.30 pm and had severed all lines of communication. A lot of the people in Southtown and Cobham had been forced out of their homes and onto the streets.

21-year-old Arthur Bensley had taken his girl friend, Carol, to see *High Noon* at the local cinema, when the manager got up on the stage to tell them of reports of furniture floating out of houses in Pier Road. Arthur lived in Pavilion Road with his mother - his father had died of cancer a few years previously - and his mother was nursing a broken arm. He was concerned for her safety, so he left Carol with a group of friends and off he ran, down the little steps in Cliff Hill. That's where he first encountered the floodwater. He had no option but to wade in; the water came up to his chest at the deepest point and he gasped in shock at the icy coldness. He waded past the local greengrocers, which was sitting in 3½ feet of water. His legs had become numb, so he decided it would be best to try and stay above the water. He climbed on to the roof of the NAAFI bakery in Beach Road that backed on to the Harbour Hotel in Pavilion Road where he lived.

Arthur Bensley on the balcony of his home, Pavilion Road, Gorleston-on-Sea, 2nd February, 1953.   *Reproduced by permission of Arthur Bensley*

He clambered across fences and jumped on to sheds and walls until he reached his back yard. He jumped back into the freezing water and opened the back door to be greeted by the sight of his mother, 11-year-old nephew, Martin, and elderly neighbour, Tom, all searching for candles as they knew the power was likely to go out. As they searched the lights went out and they were left with only the light of Arthur's torch. Arthur flashed the torch across the room and noticed the water was spurting through the keyhole and sides of the door. He grabbed what he could and had one last check with the torch through the kitchen window; the water was twelve inches up the glass pane. Arthur's mum was already going up the stairs with Martin, when the front and back doors burst simultaneously. Tom was knocked off his feet and pinned against the wall under a linen chest. Arthur helped him to his feet as the water reached waist height and they struggled upstairs, the icy water chasing after them step by step. Arthur's mind cast back to hearing of the Lynmouth floods in Devon, the previous year, and how the houses there were washed away; for the first time in his life, Arthur was terrified.

As they got settled upstairs, he remembered his elderly neighbours, two spinster sisters on one side and Mrs Clarke, a one-time Mayoress of Portsmouth, on the other. Arthur climbed over the balcony rail and hammered on the balcony door of the sisters' house.

The Little Steps, Gorleston-on-Sea, 2nd February, 1953
Reproduced by permission of Arthur Bensley

The ladies were very distressed, but he managed to help them over the rail and into his home. Then he went to get Mrs Clarke. He forced the door and ran downstairs to find her chest deep in water, dressed in her nightdress and clinging to the broken front door frame; the force of the water had burst the door off its hinges. "Dear God, save me!" wailed Mrs Clarke. Arthur helped her upstairs and found her some dry clothes to put on before helping her into his house.

Arthur Bensley, Carol Bensley, Arthur's mother.

Reproduced with the permission of Arthur Bensley

17

Pavilion Road, Gorlestone-on-Sea, looking south. 1st February, 1953

Pavilion Road, Gorleston-on-Sea, 1st February, 1953
Both photographs by permission of Arthur Bensley

Gorleston-on-Sea, floods (on left) receding in the morning of 1st February, 1953
Photograph by permission of Arthur Bensley

Water cascading over the barriers at St Philipsland, Netherlands

Chapter Four

Flooding of Harwich and Great Yarmouth
Warning signs in Southend and Canvey Island

<u>10.15 pm - Harwich, Essex</u>
Built on a small peninsula edging out into the Stour Estuary, this little harbour town was being attacked from three sides by water pouring over the quaysides, to the north, east and west. The pier had become submerged and the flood was now surging down the streets of Harwich in waves. The sea poured into gardens below street level and was carrying an enormous amount of debris that it had picked up along the way. People ran screaming as water burst into their homes. Within minutes 3,000 people were homeless and stood shivering in the cold seawater that had washed through the houses and left them in 3 feet of salt water.

As the tide sped through the streets a man who was clambering over a wall to safety spotted a young mother and child clinging to a fence below. He climbed back down and called out to the woman to give him her hand, so he could pull them both up, but she was frozen with fear. Eventually she reached out to him and the three of them got ready to climb up the wall. But a piece of furniture, speeding along with the fierce current charged into them and swept all three to their deaths.

The landlord of the Anchor Public House and his wife are in the cellar trying to salvage the smaller barrels of beer, when they hear an almighty roar. Water bursts through all three doors and begins to fill the cellar. The woman is swept upstairs by the water that slams the cellar door behind her, trapping her husband in 15 feet of water and he drowns.

Frogman in Harwich High Street

In two separate houses, on the ground floors, are two ladies that are bedridden. One awoke to see the murky saltwater smash into her bedroom and sat dumbstruck at the shock of such a terrifying spectacle, unable to scream out for help as the water swirls up past her shoulders and over her head. The other lady had a bottle on her bedside table that read 'Sleeping Tablets'; she never even flinched as the water crept over her body and smothered her as she slept soundly.

Harwich High Street after the Storm

At nearby Parkeston Quay, where the locals had earlier been holding their ambulance competitions, the water had engulfed the railway embankment. The station's Goods Yard and Locomotive Depot were all under water. Half a mile of track had been washed away at Dovercourt, and at Frinton-on-Sea and Walton-on-the-Naze the beach huts had been ripped from their foundations and dragged out to sea.

Walton-on-the-Naze caravan park

10.20 pm - Shoeburyness, Essex
At the mouth of the Thames Estuary, a huge Norwegian tanker, *Kosmos V*, had been blown off course and her captain and crew were desperately trying to stop her heading for the sands at Shoeburyness. The gales and huge waves won easily and ran her aground.

10.30 pm - Maldon, Essex
The promenade bathing pool was filled to its 2.5 million gallon capacity in just 12 minutes. The River Blackwater and the River Crouch had both burst their banks and the sea was already saturating the farmland; barns, grazing pasture and cropland all ruined in a matter of minutes.

10.40 pm - Canvey Island, Essex
The bridge attendant was approaching his little hut on the Canvey side of the bridge. He always came on duty 3 hours before high tide. It was deadly quiet, only the howling of the wind could be heard. The sky was clear and you could see a billion stars pinpricked in nights black cloak. The moon, full brightly glowing disc, lit the way; but the attendant kept his head down and his collar up to shield him from the winds icy blasts. He opened the door of the hut and entered, shivering. He lit the paraffin heater and stood rubbing his hands together. He turned to look out over the creek and held his breath, for out of the window he could see the creek was already full of water. He stepped out of the hut and ran to look at the tide marker. The saltings were already covered and, sure enough, the marker was at the '9 foot' mark. Full tide wasn't due for another 3 hours and the tide was still rising.

11 pm - Great Yarmouth, Norfolk
The River Breydon's wall gives way to the massive weight of water, sending a wall of water crashing onto the already waterlogged town. As the sleet and snow swept across the marshes the signalman in his box, near Southtown Railway Station, was knocked to the floor as the water hits the stilts of the box, shaking it violently.

In Cobholm and Southtown people are clambering to higher ground. The elderly are drowned in their beds and many die of the shock of being faced with water smashing into their homes. One woman wrapped her arms and legs around the ironwork of her bed as the water swirled up over her head. Rescuers couldn't get to her in time.

Corpses of livestock litter the marshes and a sow and her piglet are seen heading to safety along a wrecked rail track.

11 pm - Southend Pier, Southend-on-Sea, Essex
The duty officer and the pier officials decide to close the pier, as the water crept higher and higher towards the deck. The dance officials closed the dance early and sent the partygoers off home for an early night.

11.20 pm - Canvey Island, Essex
A telephone call from Harwich Harbourmaster is taken at Long Road police station. A flood warning was given and reports of flooding in Harwich itself. The police sergeant on duty decided to investigate the tide level for himself and drove over to Leigh Beck where he met the duty officer near the call box at the Admiral Jellicoe Public House. They both go to look

over the sea wall at the end of Seaview Road but don't see any cause for alarm. The sergeant asks the police officer to keep an eye out and returns to the station.

<u>11.40 pm - Southend Pier, Southend-on-Sea, Essex</u>
As the last of the partygoers left the Pier Ballroom, the wind was wild. It played havoc with the ladies' dresses, much to the amusement of the boys! As the Canvey coach party pulled away, the Southend Inspector for the Port of London Authority arrived to monitor the situation. When the duty officer showed him the tide level the inspector was horrified. He told the officer to alert Southend Police, who would in turn alert Scotland Yard. The Inspector then set about getting loudspeaker warnings issued, not just for the Esplanade, but also all the way to Leigh-on-Sea and further inland.

<u>11.50 pm - Canvey Island, Essex</u>
At Waterside farm, a few hundred yards away from the Canvey Bridge, the farmer, Fred Leach was also the Chairman of the Canvey Island Urban District Council and a member of the River Board. Fred was still up as he had received a couple of 'flood watch' warnings from the River Board and Southend police. Another call came in from an engineer at the Essex River Board depôt in Upminster. He relayed a call he had received from the Harwich Harbourmaster and told Fred of the terrible flooding there. He warned him to keep an eye on the situation.

Fred Leach pulled his boots on and went out to see what the tide level was in Benfleet Creek, which ran under the Canvey Bridge. The bridge attendant, who seemed to be in a bit of a panic, met him. Water was now washing over the road and Fred watched as it washed over his feet. Fred told the attendant to get the flood boards out and ran back to telephone Canvey police. The sergeant was shocked to hear of the water cascading down the road at Waterside Farm. Fred then tried to alert the Island's Surveyor, Reg Stevens; it was important that he knew of the flooding, but there was no answer. Fred ran back out to the bridge to help the attendant put up the boards.

The Canvey coach party were singing merrily as they drove past the Anchor Public House in Benfleet. As they reached the Half Crown and Hoy and Helmet public houses, there was a great splashing sound and the coach slowed. The passengers were quiet now as they peered out of the windows to see the flooded street.

The bridge attendant and Fred Leach heard the coach coming and waved it across. The coach drove slowly over the submerged bridge, the shocked passengers staring out of the windows at the two men holding the flood boards. The backseat passengers knelt up on the seats, as the coach drove on to the island, and watched in silence as the men struggled to secure the last boards, sealing off the island.

The coach stopped in the High Street and as the people began to walk home, some came across people leaving the War Memorial Hall. The members of the coach party told the other islanders how they had seen the floodwater at the Benfleet crossing and one man commented on how the dyke system seemed to be bursting with water; the dykes were the old Dutch drainage system, used to reclaim the land. These people still saw no cause for alarm and they broke up in separate groups to wander home.

A priest from Our Lady of Canvey Catholic Church had been to visit a sick parishioner over near Tewkes Creek that evening and was returning to his car, when he saw water spilling over the sea wall, glistening under the full moon. Suddenly, there was an almighty splashing of water and the priest jumped in his car, speeding off into Furtherwick Road. He parked his car by the Rio Cinema and used the nearby call box to alert his housekeeper and told her to ring the parishioners. He then ran back towards Tewkes Creek to start banging on doors.

The Tewkes Creek dam and new sea wall

A local photographer and his son were out for a stroll along the foot of Tewkes Creek sea wall. They stopped for a moment to shelter from the harsh icy winds, when water began flowing over the top of the wall. After a moment of stunned silence they ran off, shouting to wake the sleeping residents.

Remains of sea wall at Tewkes Creek protecting Sunken Marsh (Kellington Road).
New sea wall is set much further back.

Tewkes Creek is situated on the north-eastern side of the island. The sea wall protected an area known as Sunken Marsh (re-named today as Newlands). The rows of 24 little streets, edged by Kellington Road, Dovervelt Road, Hindles Road, and Munsterberg Road, were built on a deep marsh, well below sea level and surrounded by an earth and clay sea wall. The large majority of properties on the island were 'shack-like' chalet-bungalows, with an outer staircase to the attic room or simply a flat roof. One man, who worked for the River Board, was standing at his back door when he noticed something glistening up on the sea wall. Upon closer inspection, to his horror, he discovered that the tide was not only spilling slowly over the wall, but a small channel had formed where the seawater was beginning to creep through. He ran to wake his family and got them up into the loft space to safety and ran to the house of a neighbour, who also worked for the River Board. The two men ran down their street, banging on doors and shouting to wake people.

Newlands

New sea wall protecting Sunken Marsh, bordering Kellington Road at Tewkes Creek

Chapter Five

The flooding of Felixstowe, Kent, Leigh-on-Sea, Southend-on-Sea, Bramble Island, Jaywick, Coryton, Foulness Island, Potton Island, Great Wakering, Canvey Island, Purfleet, Tilbury and Wallasea Island

<u>Sunday, 1st February, 1953</u>

<u>12 Midnight - Felixstowe, Suffolk</u>
In the pitch black, the sound of thundering water and screaming women was terrifying. The flood was relentless; it rose higher and higher, as if it was never going to stop. People were scrambling for their lives on to the roofs of their prefabricated homes, as the water slammed into them at the Orford Road/Langer Road junction. Safe up on their roofs, they thought they were out of harm's way. They sat shivering and crying in the darkness, wearing only their nightclothes. They could see only what the moonlight picked out and they could hear terrified people trapped in their homes, shouting and screaming for help. Suddenly, they could feel the water swirling at their feet once again as the water swelled over roof level and their lives were in danger once more. They stood up, desperately looking around for somewhere higher to climb to, but within seconds, dozens of people were swept off their feet by the foaming waters and they all disappeared into the night; their screams fading into the distance.

Its track washed away, the Wivenhoe-Brightlingsea railway line hangs in the air

12 Midnight - Kent

The entire Thames front was taking the full force of the gales. Just after midnight the Kent River Board received a call from the Anglo-Iranian Oil Company at the Isle of Grain. An official warned of water pouring into the refinery from over the top of the sea wall. The weight of the mighty river breached the sea defences in numerous towns and villages, from Birchington to Woolwich, almost simultaneously.

Seawater gushed through over 400 gaps torn in the sea wall and flooded 50,000 acres of Kent farmland. Some of the towns lay under 9 feet of water. Dartford Power Station became flooded as water surged through huge gaps in the riverbank. Two explosions, blowing out the windows of shops and houses, rocked Dartford town; this had been caused by the water flooding into the local fireworks factory at Long Reach. The staff at Northfleet Paper Mills rowed to safety in boats and watched as massive reels of paper floated across the river towards Essex. In Gordon Gardens at Gravesend, the statue in the park stood waist deep in water.

At Sheerness Quayside, a great tidal wave swept in and filled the submarine *Sirdar* to a depth of 36 feet, sinking it rapidly. The frigate H.M.S. *Berkeley Castle* was capsized. - her stern in the water and her bow lifted high on to the dock. The island was almost totally submerged, foaming waves continued to batter the fragile coastline.

Towns such as Whitstable and Herne Bay became smothered in thousands of tons of shingle, washed up from the beaches. The road that connected Thanet Way with the village of Seasalter had become blocked with the bodies of dead sheep; Seasalter itself was totally destroyed. Margate town was badly damaged and the 60 foot lighthouse on Margate's Harbour jetty, fell into the sea. The electricity in the town had failed everywhere, except Dreamland Fun Park, where they had their own power plant.

12 year-old Colin Ash was living in a house in west Minster on the Isle of Sheppey, with his mother and grandmother. His mother woke him as water began pouring into the house. He could hear all the ships in Sheerness Dockyard hooting and the sirens were wailing. The local postmaster, Mr Burnett, was out in the streets shouting and hollering to wake people. The postmaster also ran a general store in the village and the seawater had destroyed all his stock.

12 Midnight - Leigh-on-Sea, Essex
The tide level was rising by the minute along the Southend coastline, in the Thames Estuary. The water crept through the row of cockle sheds, silently, and over the towpath that ran eastwards through Chalkwell and Westcliff-on-Sea. In a matter of minutes water was pouring into Leigh-on-Sea Railway Station.

12 Midnight - Bramble Island, Essex

Water had begun to flood the islands between Walton on the Naze and Harwich. At the Explosives and Chemical Products Company situated on tiny Bramble Island in the Walton Backwaters, the night watchman tried to get to safety, out of the water that was waist deep and rising. He tripped over an object hidden by the water and was unable to get up, pushed down by the fierce current. His body drifted towards Felixstowe where it would be recovered a month or so later.

12.30 am - Jaywick, Essex

The town's residents sleep peacefully, unaware of the water beginning to overtop the sea wall and cascading over.

Water and mud in Jaywick

12.40 am - Canvey Island, Essex

Fred Leach answered the hammering on his farmhouse door. It was the bridge attendant, looking very worried. He told Fred to come and look at the flood boards and he discovered that the creek had now surpassed their 3.5 feet height and was now flowing over the top. Fred sprung into action; he began 'phoning everyone. He still couldn't get hold of Reg Stevens, so he telephoned the police sergeant and asked him to call in to Reg's house in Leigh Road at the seafront end of Furtherwick Road. After contacting the Canvey Drainage Commissioner, living in Chamberlain Avenue, Fred set about waking his farm workers to help move the livestock and rouse the residents of Waterside and Sixty Acres. Waterside Farm's dairy sheds were already sitting in a good deal of water and the farm workers released the distressed cattle, herding them up to higher ground.

The Drainage Commissioner contacted another colleague to come in a car to get him, so that the men could go and inspect the sea wall at Small Gains Creek.

The police sergeant bangs on the door at Reg Stevens' house. Reg had come home early that night after feeling unwell and gone straight to bed. The sergeant briefed Mr Stevens on the impending flood, sending Reg flying into action. After dressing and inspecting the tide level on the south of the island and seeing the water lapping a foot away from the top of the wall, Reg went to his office in Long Road and began 'phoning his workers. He then telephoned the exchange and asked them to relay any breach reports to him.

The sergeant drove to find the Leigh Beck constable and ordered him to run along the sea wall, blowing his warning whistle.

The Drainage Commissioner and his colleague climb the grassy bank at Small Gains Creek and they are shocked to discover water cascading down on to the path below.

12.50 am - Coryton, Essex

Water had breached the sea wall fronting the Purfleet Deep Wharf & Storage Company and was flooding the site rapidly until it was left sitting in 10 feet of saltwater. The Tilbury loop section of the Fenchurch Street to Shoeburyness line had disappeared under the water.

65,000 tons of raw sugar that was at the depot was ruined in an instant as the waves smothered the storage sacks. 50,000 newspaper reels floated along with the tide, mixing with paper that had floated across the Thames from Northfleet.

Other oil and petrol companies and storage facilities were also flooded causing damage that ran into tens of thousands of pounds.

1 am - Foulness Island, Potton Island and Havengore Island, Essex

The 400 people living on Foulness Island are awoken by the sound of thundering water and panicking animals, as a section of sea wall to the north of the island breaches along a mile long stretch. The people have been trapped in the upstairs of their homes. They could see out of their bedroom windows, lit by the full moon, the pigs, cattle and sheep struggling to get to dry land. As they found a patch of higher ground, so the water still came and began to rise high above it, forcing the animals to swim for their lives again and again. For some poor animals it became too much and they drowned in the deep water, watched helplessly by the farmers. Many sheep drown as they became entangled in fences, their feet getting caught in the wires, hidden by the flood. Game birds flew into trees, alongside rabbits that had been flooded out of their warrens and clambered to safety.

St Mary the Virgin, Foulness, 2nd February

One man, a retired police officer, was awoken by water surging into his bedroom. He found a boathook to stop the current dragging him away and walked to Courtsend to try and wake the residents.

The eleven residents living in the three farm cottages on Potton Island are safe on the first floors of their homes. The only residents of Havengore Island were the island's only farmer and his family and the Havengore Bridge keeper and his family. The War Department police had an office called Taylor's Hut on the island and only one constable was there on duty that night. He saw the flood coming and ran to alert the farmer, the bridge keeper was already aware of the situation and had taken his family into the first floor bedrooms of their cottage to safety. The constable returned to Taylor's Hut after waking the farmer, to make a report to his H.Q.. As the water filled the tiny building, even on the first floor, the constable found himself marooned on the flat roof and there he prepared to spend a terribly cold night.

1 am - Wallasea Island, Essex
The landlady of the Creeksea Ferry Inn, Mrs Ivy Taylor-Smith, telephones her friend, living in Thorpe Bay, to tell her that they were knee deep in floodwater in the bar. The friend was worried and contacted Rochford Police.

1 am - Great Wakering, Essex

Situated on the low-laying village common was one of two abandoned WW II Nissen hut army camps, the other being in Alexander Road. They were being used to temporarily house people while they waited for more suitable accommodation from Rochford Council. This camp was known as 'Home Farm Camp' and was made up of 34 arched corrugated iron huts, housing 112 people. Water came crashing in at Morrins Point, where the sea wall had burst under the enormous amount of pressure from the weight of the water pressing against it. The residents were awoken by a torrent of water bursting into their homes and though still half asleep most manage to get themselves and their children outside to seek higher ground. The water was rising rapidly as the people waded, waist deep, with their children on their shoulders. As the water deepened, so the current got stronger. This un-eased many of the residents; one woman put her 3 year-old boy on to the windowsill of one of the huts and began to climb up herself. Soon the others were doing the same and they all found themselves climbing high up on to the slippery arched roofs to keep out of the ice cold rising water. There they are in their nightclothes that were soaking wet from wading in the freezing saltwater, being battered by the gale force winds that threatened to toss them into the wild waters below.

One elderly couple found it too difficult to try and climb up on to the roof. They managed to get their disabled son up safely, but the woman physically couldn't climb the awkward arched roof. The couple decide to get back inside their home and stood on the stove. The people outside could hear them singing 'Abide With Me' as the waters rose higher and higher, until there was silence.

The young mum with her 3 year-old boy saw a floating dining table and managed to grab it as it came past. She put her toddler on the upturned table and realising she might tip it up if she got on, decided to get into the water and push it from behind; but the current of water between the huts was deadly and a wave separated her from the table. She desperately tried to swim after the fast moving table, but it was impossible. As some people pulled her from the water to safety, she could only weep hysterically as she watches her crying child disappear into the darkness.

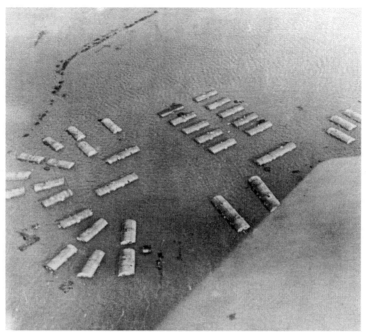

The Great Wakering Nissen huts

The local police constable had seen the water pouring into the camp and ran to the call box at the eastern end of the High Street to report the flooding to his police station. He ran to ring the fire alarm, but the power had gone out and he found himself cycling to the house of the nearest fire officer to raise the alarm. Another man who had witnessed the flooding had already got a little boat and was rowing out the submerged huts to try and rescue the families stranded on the roofs. He was only able to take one or two passengers at a time due to the size of his boat and the fact that conditions were atrocious; the wind and waves tossed the boat about making the journey hazardous.

1 am - Southend-on-Sea and Leigh-on-Sea, Essex

600 Southend homes were flooded and to make matters worse, the electrics were short circuiting and bursting into flames, setting houses alight and making the fire brigade's already painstaking job of rescuing people, a lot harder. Two elderly men died as a result of the water flooding into their homes in Victoria Road and Burnaby Road, behind the domed building of Kursaal Amusements on Eastern Esplanade. One of the men died of bronchial pneumonia and the other simply from shock.

The tide had swallowed up the entire seafront. Southchurch Park had turned into a giant lake and Peter Pan's Playground had vanished beneath the water level, only the upper level of the Crooked House was visible. Old Leigh's little terraced cottages and pubs, the Smack Inn, the Peter Boat and the Crooked Billet were all sitting in 3½ feet of lashing seawater. The residents, who had grown accustomed to flooding during the 'spring tides' were well prepared and had taken refuge on the first floor of their properties.

A 'phone call was taken at Southend police station from a man saying that he and his colleague were trapped on the roof of the Two Tree Island Sewage Works, where they had been working. Then the 'phone lines went down and the whole area was in darkness with no communication.

1 am - Jaywick, Essex

At nearby St Osyth, the flood defences burst at the mouth of the Colne Estuary, sending vast amounts of saltwater hurtling across the marshes towards sleeping Jaywick. The little town, built almost entirely at sea level, was still unaware of the water, which was still pouring over the sea wall. The residents didn't stand a chance. They were blocked in from all sides by the raging flood and the sea mercilessly washes their homes away.

A disabled woman, 42 year old Miss Marie Miles, awoken by the water flooding into her home telephones the young Reeves family nearby to warn them of the flood, so they could get to safety. Her selfless act saved their lives.

Jaywick, the morning after

Up the hill from the seafront, a man living on Beacon Hill telephones his parents, Mr and Mrs Crosswell, living in Point Clear Stores. He warns them to get out, but his terrified mother tells him to save himself, as he hears the shop windows give way and the roar of water as it flooded his parents' shop. He ran out to try and get to them, but the speed of the water was deadly and he wouldn't have stood a chance. His parents were another two people to add to the growing list of flood victims.

Jaywick, 1st February, 1953 *The Len Whittaker Collection*

2,000 million gallons of water swamped the streets, entering houses and was a metre high within 15 minutes and continuing to rise. The Brooklands housing estate was completely savaged by the ferocity of the water, leaving 700 people homeless and running through the flooded streets. The little holiday chalets made of wood are slammed by the wind and waves, the timber splintered and snapped like matchsticks and was thrown about the town and back out to sea. The caravans at Tower Camp suffered much the same fate as they are tossed upside down and many float away.

Mid-Way, Jaywick. *The Len Whittaker Collection*

There were 600 people now being dragged along with the surge or trapped in their homes, all desperately clinging to debris. A further 100 people were already safe as they had found higher ground. 35 people, some 5% of Jaywick's population, became the storm's next victims, most drowning in their beds. The town had become like a sequence from a nightmare. The water was calmer now; only the biting wind and crying children pierced the otherwise deadly silence. Men, women, and children were stranded on rooftops, wardrobes, windowsills, and tables. They were all soaking wet and freezing cold. They all knew they may have survived the sea's relentless onslaught, but would they survive the exposure to the elements as they waited for rescuers to come?

1.10 am - Canvey Island, Essex

The Drainage Commissioner and his colleague were inspecting the length of Small Gains sea wall and could hear a whistle blowing up ahead. It was one of the River Board workers, running towards them. Then there was a movement in the grass up ahead; the wall was beginning to collapse. The drainage workers start shouting to try and warn people, but it was all so tragically sudden. The wall crumbles, sending millions of gallons pouring into Sunken Marsh and Newlands in a deafening roar. The residents have seconds to escape.

Over on Tewkes Creek was a houseboat named *Tideways*, occupied by a Dutch family; Kars and Gertrude Prium and their 8 year-old son. Mr Prium had stayed awake to monitor the water level in case his houseboat was in danger of going over the wall. He witnessed the wall at Tewkes Creek giving way and ran along the wall shouting to wake the residents. He could see the River Board workers, who had been banging on doors, scrambling for their lives. They were still shouting, one had found a couple of dustbin lids to bang together, anything to wake their sleeping neighbours.

One resident is woken from his slumber to see a huge wave bursting down his bedroom door. In shock from the icy temperature of the water, he struggles upstairs, with the water chasing after him up every step. He ran to the window to look out to the street below and was dumbstruck by the scene before him. There were caravans floating down the street accompanied by sheds, timber, and all sorts of broken debris. The wind and waves smashed them into the walls and windows of houses. The noise was unbearably loud.

Even the people who were warned of the impending flood were finding it difficult to escape the relentless speed of the flood. The water level outside was much higher than inside, owing to the rapid speed in which the water was rising. Many people could see the water lapping halfway up their windows and didn't want to risk being mown down by a wall of water as they opened their front doors. These people chose to seek refuge by standing on stoves and wardrobes, as water oozed through gaps in doors and window frames, until help arrived.

One couple are woken by their dog barking and realised their lives were in danger. Their bungalow was flat roofed and the father smashed a hole out through the ceiling to get out and pull his wife and kids through. Their eldest daughter lived a few hundred yards away and was married with a new baby. They were trapped on the veranda and neither of them could swim. They tucked their 8-week-old baby girl into her Moses basket as the waters rose and the husband told his wife to get up on his shoulders. He tried to walk to find.a place of safety, but it is believed that he tripped and fell causing them both to drown. His body bent over the veranda, which is where rescuers would find the tragic couple, still locked together. Their baby bobbed safely in her Moses basket.

By 1.30 the water had raced much further across the island, disturbing a 7-month pregnant woman, as it crashed against the side of their bungalow. She woke her husband to get him to investigate the strange noises outside and as he went to the window he saw the water creeping up the glass pane and felt its icy coldness as it oozed up through the floorboards. He ran to the door and pulled the bolt open, water crashed in sending him flying. The couple ran outside and could see the water charging down the street. The woman, despite her delicate condition, climbed next door's fence and they both climbed the shaky wooden staircase on the outside of their neighbour's bungalow. After hammering on the door, they were let in and spent the night there.

The people of Canvey were, like every other town, taken completely by surprise. One man resorted to throwing water over his wife to get her out of bed, as she thought he was sleep walking and told him to get back in bed!

The baby crying woke a family living at Central Wall. When the mother reached out to comfort the child, she couldn't feel his crib. When she switched on the bedside lamp she discovered him floating across the room. There was no time to lose as the water level rose. She woke her husband and two little girls as the front door burst open with the force of water. The husband managed to close the door and the wife decided to go and swim for help. The water outside far too powerful for her to swim in and she ended up grabbing the banister to their outer staircase and running up to the attic room to find sheets to knot together so that she could pull her children and husband up to safety. Her husband is the last to be rescued and is almost dragged away with the surge as it passes the top of the window level.

Andrew, Chris, Graham, and Malcolm Manser were awoken by their eldest brother, Ian, who told them to get up and out of bed quickly. Dazed and confused as to why they should have to get out of their lovely warm beds, the boys did as they were told and began to get out from under the covers. As Andrew and Chris swung their legs out of the beds, they felt the icy-cold water grabbing at their legs. Unable to dress, as all their clothes were on a pile on the floor under the water, the boys waded through the icy water and struggled up the two steps from their bedroom, to get to the lounge. Wearing nothing but their vests the boys found their parents with the four youngest children and Ian and waited to be told what to do next as the water rose steadily higher. The gas mantle had been lit and it was reassuring to be able to see what was going on.

Mr Manser sent Ian to swim the short distance to the sea wall, as he was a good swimmer, and run and get help; Rufus, the family's beloved mongrel dog, followed him. The doors were slid shut behind him so as to try and prevent the water from coming in so quickly. Next, Mr Manser began smashing a hole in the ceiling, so he could help everyone get up into the loft space. As he did this, he brushed against the mantle, causing the main flame to go out and left them with only the naked blue flame. Mr and Mrs Manser decided quickly that it would be dangerous to leave the flame like that and so Mr Manser turned off the gas tap, plunging the room into total darkness. Matches were lit occasionally, but these soon burned out or got wet. The six remaining children and Mr Manser were all sitting up in the attic, with strict instructions to stay on the joists, as the ceiling panels wouldn't take their weight. Mrs Manser decided there wasn't enough room in the attic for her and the two babies so she stayed in the lounge. Mr Manser began to worry about his wife being in the water, so she opened the window that opened out into the veranda and sat on the sill, one leg in the lounge and one in the veranda, while she held tightly on to the handle of the babies' floating pram. Everyone, amazingly, remained very calm.

Reg Stevens, the Island's Surveyor, was contacted by the exchange who informed him of numerous breach reports at Tewkes Creek and Small Gains and that the water was windowsill high. Mr Stevens was stunned; he contacted the fire brigade immediately and sent them to begin the rescue operation.

As the fire engine drove down Chamberlain Avenue, sounding the siren, the appliance drove into deep water, so deep in fact that the firemen had no option but to turn back and report in. No one seemed to be taking any notice of the siren and Reg Stevens told them to fire some maroons. Mr Stevens then contacted Chelmsford Police HQ to request back up and asked for boats and ambulances to be sent. The police contacted Colchester Barracks to send in the army. Leigh Beck School was opened a the first rescue centre and people so far unaffected by the water dressed and came out to lend a hand. It was mayhem, but organised and well executed mayhem. The people of Canvey Island had found themselves in a situation of an extremely deadly nature.

Over at Tewkes Creek, Kars Prium was still running along the wall and shouting to wake people. On the wind was carried the terrified screams of women and children as they fought for their lives against the strong and icy cold current of the water. You could hear people calling, mixed in with the dreadful racket of debris, smashing against walls, doors, and windows.

1.40 am - Rochford District, Essex

The constable at Rochford police station left with the sergeant to go and investigate the flood report on Wallasea Island. The constable on duty covering Stambridge, Canewdon, and Paglesham was off sick that night. They were held up briefly on their way by a man they found lying unconscious in the road! They radioed in for assistance and continued on towards Wallasea Island.

Lion Creek had flooded the road leading on to Wallasea Island, as it always did during a 'spring tide'. The policemen knocked on the door of a nearby farm to speak to the farmer, who thought they should all row over to Wallasea in his boat, just to check on the flood level, but the sergeant didn't see this as necessary and said he would return at daybreak. Before returning to the station they checked on the situation at Paglesham, but again saw no cause for alarm.

The farmer at Creeksea was concerned and decided to keep an eye on things from the upstairs window of his farmhouse. He sat down just in time to see a huge amount of water surge up Lion Creek and flood over his precious farmland.

1.40 am - Felixstowe, Suffolk

Coastguard John Dobson found a rowing boat and using two shovels as oars, he rowed down to the prefab estate and began rescuing people. He plucks 24 people off the rooftops and rows them to safety.

<u>1.45 am - Tilbury, Essex</u>

The water had risen to a level of 4 feet against the walls of the Tilbury and Riverside General Hospital. The patients were in the process of being told to prepare to be taken to the docks where a ship would evacuate them. Unknown to them the tide was on the turn and on ebb, the water that had earlier flooded parts of the town from the dock tidal basin, was now flowing back into the Thames. Within minutes Tilbury town was 3 feet under water and the water was still coming. Police officers on duty, two sergeants and six constables, were running through the streets with some residents, shouting and blowing whistles to wake people. They helped the old and disabled seek higher shelter and one of the policemen found a little boy wandering through the streets. The boy was looking for his dog that had run out of the house in fear as the water flooded in. As they spoke, the dog floated past on a big cake tray!

Civic Square, Tilbury

In one house, a 79 year-old lady had gone into her downstairs toilet just before the water flooded in. The water pinned the door firmly shut and left her screaming for help. Her frailty, coupled with the pressure of the water, prevented her from being able to open the door and she eventually drowned.

Somewhere around 2,500 homes out of 2,750 in the town, were flooded to a depth of 5 feet. 10,000 people were trapped in the upstairs of their houses and they sat and listened to the police Public Address cars as they warned people not to flush their toilets, as the local sewage plant was flooded and raw sewage could pump out into the streets if there was any rush of water.

1.50 am - Canvey Island, Essex

Sub-Officer Frank Griffiths was sounding the siren again and still no one seemed to take any notice. Then he had an idea; the Sub-Officer decided to dip the pitch of the siren to make it sound like an Air-Raid Warning! Sure enough people got up out of bed to investigate the cause for the siren and were met by an ice-cold footbath, alerting them to the danger. If the siren hadn't been sounded this way maybe many more lives would have been lost on the island, as people would have continued to ignore the fire siren.

1.50 am - West Minster, Kent

Colin Ash's house, in Cromwell Avenue, was now sitting in 5 feet of freezing cold water, but the other end of the village was in much deeper water. The houses in Terence Road were flooded up to the bedroom windows.

2 am - Creeksea, Essex

The residents of Creeksea joined hands as they waded through the raging water that was flooding into their homes. The only needed to walk 5 or 6 feet over to some farm buildings where they took refuge in a hayloft until rescuers came.

2 am - Wallasea Island, Essex

Ivy Taylor-Smith, the landlady of the Ferry Inn on the south side of the River Crouch, and three of her customers had run out to the car park to try and escape the rising water. Realising they wouldn't make it to safety the group turn back to climb up on to the roof of the inn. Mrs Taylor-Smith decides to go back inside to fetch her coat and one of the customers, Charles Rolfe, accompanies her inside, carrying a torch. As the pair turned to wade back outside to climb on the roof, they saw that the water was halfway up the glass on the outside of the main door and was spraying through the cracks. They both ran back into the inn and climbed on a table near one of the inner doors. As the water burst through, the table was swept from under their feet leaving them clinging to the top of the door. The man told the landlady to support herself by putting a foot on to the door handle and to push herself up.

After a while it became clear that Mr Rolfe was struggling to hold on to the door and he told the landlady that he was going to swim and get help. That was the last time anyone saw him alive. He left the landlady alone in total darkness with the water level just under her chin, as she held on to the top of the door; it would be hours before she was rescued by Colonel B Carey of Raymonds Farm, who had become concerned and launched his pram dinghy at 4 a.m. and rowed downstream alone. He took all the people in the Ferry Inn to the sea-wall and then rowed Mrs Taylor-Smith to hospital. For his rescue work Colonel Carey was later awarded the M.B.E.

Water flooding through Norpits near Wallasea on 4th February

Wallasea, the morning after

Chapter Six

The first rescues as the water subsides;
Canvey Island, Sea Palling, Great Wakering,
Foulness Island, Wallasea Island and Hunstanton

2 am - Canvey Island, Essex

Numerous calls came into the switchboard at Long Road police station with the voices of terrified people screaming for help or giving warning of the charging floodwater.

As the water crept into Canvey village, young George Thain was on home leave from National Service in the army. His mother came into his bedroom to wake him and said, "George! Wake up, it's flooded!"

George replied, "Flooded? What do you mean 'flooded'?" and he got out of bed to investigate. Sure enough, their bungalow was sitting in 2 inches of ice-cold saltwater.

Realising that other parts of the island could be under much deeper water, George decided to find a boat and go out to see if he could find anyone that needed help. To look at, Canvey seems to be completely flat, but the flood made everyone realise that this was not the case. The water seemed to be ranging from a shallow wash over of about 2 inches to deadly depths of 10 feet. George saw numerous dead bodies, but carried on his search for the living. Terrified barking dogs that wouldn't allow people to get into the flooded properties were hampering rescue missions. One bungalow that George entered had the biggest and fiercest Alsatian he had ever seen; it bobbed up and down on the kitchen table with its head knocking against the ceiling where the water had risen so high. The family trapped behind the dog couldn't even calm the poor thing down!

Kars Prium ran back to his houseboat and told his wife that he was going out to try and rescue the people trapped in the Sunken Marsh. She told him to bring them back to the houseboat where she would get them warm and give them hot tea to drink. As Gertrude searched their home for all the clean sheets, blankets and towels, Kars rowed out among the almost submerged bungalows shouting out to anyone who needed help. Families were huddled together on rooftops and he could hear the muffled cries of people trapped in their homes. He so desperately wanted to rescue them all, so he began the gruelling task of helping the shocked cold and scared people on to his boat. After leaving them with his wife, he went out again and again filling up his houseboat.

2 am - Sea Palling, Norfolk

The family and neighbours trapped on their roof could see that the water had receded enough for them to climb down. Furniture was hanging from the trees and all sorts of wildlife sat silently in the branches. All of the women and the father were feeling the effects of hypothermia, especially the elderly next-door neighbour; she had become rigid with cold, so they lay her on a table nearby and rubbed her arms and legs to warm her. Within a few minutes they saw beams from torches coming their way; it was some of the men from the village. They told the group to walk with them to a nearby rescue centre that had been set up and warned them to keep well to the right of the sand dunes as they walked.

The walk was terrifying, they walked waist deep in the freezing water and there were hidden obstacles to fall over and potholes to fall into. The dunes had been totally washed away and the water to the left of them was dangerously deep. The father suffered a huge stroke on the way and threw himself into a nearby boat to die. The mother had almost given up hope and the daughter resorted to lifting her mother's legs for her, step by step, and was met with a face-full of icy saltwater that made her choke, would they ever get to the rescue centre? The young girl eventually passed out and awoke to find herself in the rescue centre with her mother, father, family friend and the elderly neighbour and her daughter. They had all barely survived the great flood. Her father had been seen falling into the boat and was rescued by a villager.

As dawn approached, tens of thousands of people along Britain's east coast face hours of waiting on rooftops, exposed to the sharp icy winds that blasted them as they waited to be rescued. A massive percentage of them had already been in the water and were dressed in soaking wet nightclothes or naked. The people that didn't make it outside were either safe on their first floor or standing on wardrobes, stoves, draining boards and headboards, some neck deep in freezing water and nothing to do but wait to be rescued ... and it's still pitch black and deadly cold.

Memorial bench at St Margaret's Church, Sea Palling

3 am - Zeeland and Noord-Brabant, Netherlands
The alarm bells were ringing and sirens were wailing. The sea defences could no longer take the strain from the billions of gallons of North Sea water pressurising them, and they give way. The sea surged forward, engulfing and submerging the towns and tens of thousands of people were now fighting for their lives. It mirror images the panic just a few hundred miles across the sea on Britain's east coastal towns and villages.

3 am - Canvey Island, Essex

The ambulances and police reinforcements had been waiting on the Benfleet side of the bridge for the tide level to fall so that the flood boards could be removed and the debris on the bridge to be shifted. As the flood boards are removed, the convoy makes its way to set up a base in the village. The Red Cow Public House had escaped flooding and the water lapped at the grass banks outside.

The Manser family had spent the last couple of hours singing hymns the children had learned in Sunday school. Mrs Manser used to be a tambourine girl in the Salvation Army and encouraged the children to sing as loudly and lustily as they could. The children had found that this made them feel better and happily sang along with their mother.

After a while, the children began to tire and ran out of new songs to sing. The water level had risen much higher and Mrs Manser, although still sitting on the windowsill, was waist deep. The height of the water stopped any outside noise from coming in and now the children had stopped singing there was an eerie silence. Suddenly, there was a terrible crack and a huge splash of water in the lounge. Mr Manser shouted to his children to see if they were okay, but before any of them uttered a word there was a horrifying scream of terror from below. 5 year-old Keith had fallen asleep and rolled off the joist in the attic and on to a ceiling panel, causing it to give way. He screamed and gurgled as he began to swallow the water. Mr Manser called to Chris to jump in and help his brother, which he did without hesitation. The family sat in the total darkness and listened to the terrible sounds of thrashing water, as Chris tried to get a grip on Keith, then there was silence. They all knew something terrible had happened to Keith. Chris struggled to get on to the table and then sat there with a tight grip on his little brother.

3 am - Great Wakering, Essex

The evacuation of the 112 residents of Home Farm Camp was well under way. Cottawight and Home Farm had opened their doors to give people hot drinks and a change of clothes. The whole village had sprung into action to help their flooded neighbours; the vicar had opened the church hall to receive the rescued people and there the local doctor examined them. W.V.S. ladies woke the villagers to borrow clothes and blankets and made tea. The head teacher of the local school gave all the school blankets and the local baker had a big supply of candies to light the church hall.

The fire engine was as close to the Nissen huts as it could possibly get; the rest of the journey had to be made in boats. Gwen Rawlingson was a 27 year-old woman still living at home with her parents and sisters; they were awoken by a fireman knocking on their door to ask her father if he could lend them any of his boats; Gwen's father was the local boat builder, he had a few boats of his own, plus boats he was making for individual villagers and residents of the farms on Foulness Island. The girls got up and started to get ready to go out and help people. Gwen noticed that the water had stopped rising by the village pond, but had no idea of the devastation that had occurred.

The firemen and villagers trying to rescue the people on Home Farm Camp were struggling against the terrible weather conditions; it was taking half an hour to row only 150 yards of the total 500 yards from the church to the camp. The wind and water were wild and it made rowing the boats a backbreaking task. When the people arrived at the water's edge, a fire engine drove them to the church hall; it is thought that the excitement of being in a real fire engine helped the children to recover from their ordeal a lot quicker.

At the church hall the doctor examined everyone, if he thought they needed hospital care the local fishmonger was on standby with his car. Only one ambulance arrived at the scene with a message that no more could be sent as the people of Canvey Island were literally underwater and it was feared hundreds of deaths had occurred. The landlord of the Red Lion Public House gave out shots of whiskey to warm the half frozen men and women.

3-4 am - Foulness Island, Essex
The retired policeman tried to reach the little timber cottage that his sister-in-law lived with a teacher from the school in Barling, behind the sea wall. He managed to wade out as far as Ridgemarsh, but the current was very strong here and far too dangerous. He couldn't even get to Ridgemarsh Farm to alert the occupants. He decided to leave it for a while and try again later.

5 am - Central Europe
The storm loses its momentum and finally the winds begin to ease back.

6 am - Rochford Hospital, Rochford Essex
The first casualties begin to arrive from Home Farm Camp.

6 am - Foulness Island, Essex
The retired police officer finally reached the timber cottage after several attempts only to find the teacher, but no sign of his sister-in-law; reluctantly they gave up the search for her and they both waded back to Courtsend.

6 am - Southend-on-Sea, Essex
The RSPCA office was contacted by Benfleet police to inform them of the disaster on Canvey Island and of the plight of all the trapped and drowned animals. The officer on duty heads for the island immediately.

6 am - Wallasea Island, Essex
The island sat under 4 feet of water at Creeksea and two families living in Grapnell Cottages had spent the night sheltering on their first floors after the flood came in and washed away the contents of their kitchens and lounges. One family had a 5 year-old girl and a 2 month-old baby boy and the other family had three girls, one of 11 and the other two were just 1 and 3 years old and a 13 year-old boy.

Three men from Rayleigh had heard of the flooding and decided to go out in their boat to see if they could help anyone. The families saw the men in the boats and signalled to them to come to their aid. The boat was unable to get right up to the house as the garden fence was just under the water and was barring the way. The men ended up making a pathway out of floating planks of wood that they found, so they could get to the families. The boat, unfortunately, was too small for them all to fit in, so the husbands stayed behind with the three older children while the ladies took the six little ones to head off to the mainland.

The boat was 1½ miles from the shore when they struck an underwater section of sea wall and became stuck. A cabin cruiser had also grounded out on the wall and the families and the rescuers all transferred to it as it was a larger vessel.

After a while, some men spotted them from the shore and waded out to help them. They took coats with them to wrap around the stranded people who must have been freezing cold. The men walked waist deep and often had to clamber over hidden sections of sea wall. When they reached the boats, three of the men carried the three youngest children and the other men helped the women ashore.

The fathers and children on Wallasea Island were rescued later on and all were admitted to Rochford Hospital.

6 am - South Benfleet, Essex

Bert Evans, the headmaster of Benfleet Secondary School, received a telephone call from the police, asking him if he could open his new school up in Shipwrights Drive to take in the overflow of refugees arriving from Canvey Island. Still half asleep and not realising the seriousness of the situation, he refuses. The thought of dozens of people with wet and muddy feet trampling over his new school floor didn't please him.

However, the phone call played on his mind and he became concerned. Mr Evans then decided to go down to the Benfleet Primary School to see the situation for himself. As he pulled up outside there were lorries and buses dropping off scores of people. He got out of his car and walked passed the queue of people that were half-naked and dripping wet, shuffling quietly into the school hall. Women whisked them off to tables with jumbles of old clothes piled on them, so they could get dressed into dry clothing. The headmaster couldn't believe his eyes; he drove straight up to the new school and telephoned the police, ordering them to send the next thousand islanders up to his school. Mr Evans then 'phoned around all his teachers, cleaners and secretaries to get volunteers to help out. They turned out in force, bringing bags of clothes and toys, even women who didn't have children at the school turned up.

6.30 am - Stranraer, Dumfries, Scotland

James Marshall, the railway fireman, walked up to see his friend Geordie McMillan to find out if there was any news on the fate of his friends on the *Princess Victoria* passenger ferry. Geordie was very upset and said that he was going to get on the 7 am ferry that was leaving port to go to Larne and identify his brother David's body. The stark reality that was to shatter the residents of Stranraer for many decades, was beginning to sink in. 44 of the dead were from the town, everyone knew someone who had been lost.

6.55 am - East Coast of Britain

As dawn broke, so the sun illuminated the full horror of the storm's aftermath. Hundreds of people lay dead or dying; drowned or over exposed to the harsh elements of a winter's night as they waited to be rescued in wet clothes or immersed for hours in the freezing water. The breaches in coastal defences were catastrophic; hundreds of miles of sea walls were smashed, ruined and torn away by the mighty North Sea. River walls had been squashed flat by the force of millions of gallons of water that had pressurised the banks until they broke. Thousands of livestock littered the countryside, bloated by the water their corpses had soaked up like sponges. Groups of living animals huddled pathetically on tiny patches of high ground that peak out of the water-bound islands.

The surviving humans that had survived the flood and cruel night; some passed out from the cold and slipped from their safe havens to certain death in the water below. The tide was receding and rescuers from all walks of life were still hard at work in their boats, trying to find the living and remembering where they'd seen the dead. The living came first ... you can't help the dead.

7 am - Canvey Island, Essex
The RSPCA man joined the traffic at Benfleet to get on to Canvey Island and was aghast as he approached the bridge to see that the island was virtually submerged; just the tops of the houses poking up in the distance. As he got on to the island he was ordered to help with the evacuation of the islanders until back up from the army arrived.

7.15 am - Hunstanton, Norfolk
Rescues were well underway to try and save the inhabitants from the forty little bungalows along the sea wall towards Heacham. The conditions were appalling. The wind was still quite sharp and the water was littered with all manner of debris. A contingent from USAF Sculthorpe arrived after hearing of the tragedy and the men set to work to save the stranded people, who were still clinging to anything above the water level. Before they had arrived, the rescuers consisted of the local police force, council workers and civilian volunteers; they were doing their very best to save people, but they needed more help. The Yanks were not supposed to be involved in a rescue mission, as this was not American soil. This fact was completely ignored, as far as they were concerned there were dozens of men, women, and children dying out there and they were going to do everything in their power to save them.

One of the airmen, Corporal Reis Lemming, was in his early 20s and stood well over 6 foot in height. He got kitted up in an exposure suit and walked out to the stranded people, pulling a dinghy behind him. The water was almost up to his chin! He waded out, back and forth, for a total of four hours non-stop and pulled 27 people to safety before collapsing from the cold and sheer exhaustion.

Volunteers at nearby pleasure beach had begun the horrific search for the bodies of the missing people. One man wept openly as he carried away the lifeless body of a little boy, the son of one of the US airmen who had been living in the bungalows.

The Dutch island of Texel

The Leigh-Benfleet railway line

Chapter Seven

Rescues at Great Yarmouth, Canvey Island, Leigh-on-Sea, and Great Wakering

<u>7 am - Canvey Island, Essex</u>
As light began to creep in from under the water in the Manser family home everyone could begin to make out the damage. Mrs Manser was silhouetted as she sat in the window frame, still holding onto the pram handle with the two babies inside, and Chris was standing on the table clutching Keith tightly. Mrs Manser could see inside the pram and she called out to her husband that the babies were dead.

"No, Anne, not dead, they are sleeping," he reassured her. She knew they had passed away, but she seemed to cling to what her husband had said, so desperate for her worst fears not to be true.

<u>7.30 am - Great Yarmouth, Norfolk</u>

Arthur Bensley and his family and neighbours had spent the night in the bedrooms in the upstairs of his house. They had been unable to climb out to rescue boats as the ladies were too frail and his mother had broken her arm.

His girl friend, Carol, had been waiting at the top of the White Lion Steps since first light to see if she could get any news on Arthur and his family. Arthur was thinking of Carol and decided to climb out on to the roof and wave a sheet so he could be spotted. Carol saw him and gasped a sigh of relief when she saw he was alright.

Bottom of the White Lion Steps, Gorleston-on-Sea, 2nd February, 1953

Reproduced by permission of Arthur Bensley

Carol wanted to get to Arthur and get him some provisions and candles, so in excitement she ran down the steps only to be stopped by a policeman who said, "Young lady, we're trying to get people out, not in!" Carol explained her situation to the policeman, but he was curious as to where the provisions were that she so badly wanted to get to the family. Carol realised she didn't have any money, but the policeman dug into his pockets and gave her enough money to get what she needed and then commandeered a boat to take her to Pavilion Road. She was soon reunited with Arthur.

Aldeburgh, Suffolk

8 am - Aldeburgh, Suffolk

After a night of listening to the terribly fierce wind whipping around the house, 15 year old John Lovett and his family awoke to see flood water had washed over their back garden. John was recovering from an operation to both legs and had them both encased in plaster. He watched from the lounge as his father opened the cellar doors to reveal pots and pans bobbing on the water's surface, just below the cellar ceiling. Another few inches and the sea water would have soaked up through the lounge carpet!

Aldeburgh

8 am - Colchester Army Barracks, Essex

A call came in to the office for the adjutant for 1st Essex Home Guard Battalion. The commanding officer for 'A' Company informed the adjutant of the flood situation and requested the assistance of the Home Guard to evacuate Canvey Island. Assistance was also required to evacuate Wallasea Island.

The troops were rounded up and distributed accordingly, the majority headed for Canvey Island.

8 am - Canvey Island, Essex

Over at Sixty Acres, members of the South Benfleet Yacht Club had sailed their boats over to two houses that were situated behind the inner sea wall. The wall hadn't breached here and the houses weren't flooded, but the occupants had fled to safety anyway. The girls in the group lit a fire inside one house and began to search for blankets, dry clothes and tea bags, ready to help the people that the boys were going out to rescue from their submerged bungalows.

On the Prium family's houseboat, ambulance crews and a doctor were dealing with the sick and injured. It was a tragic sight; two children lay dead in the arms of their distraught mothers, who clung to them in the hope that they were only sleeping.

564 (M) LAA Searchlight Regiment RA, TA, arrived on the island to rig up a floodlight over at Tewkes Creek to assist in operations when nightfall came. The men were shocked into silence as they gazed across the flooded island. The policeman directing traffic told them to follow the line of black blobs sticking out of the water; these were roadside posts, partially submerged. The water was halfway up the wheels of the lorry as they drove east and at time the exhaust was underwater.

When they reached Tewkes Creek and began setting up, the men had to get a generator into position against the wall. One of the men felt something knock against his leg; he looked down to see a dead woman staring up at him through the water. Close by was another body; it brought home to the soldiers the horror that the people must have been through.

At 9 am the bridge attendant finally finished his shift. He left a note for the next attendant on duty to tell him what had happened and that the bridge raising mechanism was broken. The tide level was noted at 14-15 feet.

9 am - Leigh-on-Sea, Essex

The fishermen were busy cleaning up their sheds in Cockle Row at the western end of the High Street in the 'old town', from where the tide had swept through their businesses. They were all shocked to see that the railway station had been flooded out; even though they were used to flooding, the tide had never come up that far before.

A couple of fishermen decided to go and check on the boats moored in the creek between Leigh and Two Tree Island. They discovered the two men who had tried to contact the police during the night, sitting on the roof of the sewage works. They helped them down and rowed them to Leigh.

The scene at the Red Cow Public House in the village was like something from a movie set; hundreds of people that had been rescued from rooftops and attics, huddled on the grass verge by the roadside. They waited patiently for rescue vehicles to take them to refuge centres in nearby Benfleet.

The army had begun to arrive in droves and were guided to the Red Cow by the Police Chief Superintendent. 'Operation Canute' was brought into action and the troops were distributed across the island to begin with the rescue efforts; most troops were sent to the Sunken Marsh where thousands were still trapped. These soldiers used the Admiral Jellicoe public house, in the High Street, as a base. Army lorries that could be driven through deep water were sent to ferry the people back to the Red Cow, where they would then wait for evacuation.

A sweeping evacuation was ordered from The Point, along the High Street and all roads south of the High Street. All the houses were to be checked thoroughly, the soldiers were reminded that most victims would probably be in the bedrooms of the properties, as they would have been in bed at the time of the flooding. The soldiers were also ordered to leave the dead, but make note of where they were seen; the living came first. The soldiers waded through the freezing water, calling out to the residents before entering the properties to do a full search. No boats were available at this time due to the urgency and water depth over at Sunken Marsh.

10 am - Aldeburgh, Suffolk

A family friend took John Lovett in a car to assess flood damage to the town. The river wall had breached at Slaughden and flooded the marshes. The shingle bank between the Martello Tower and the local Yacht Club had burst, sending sea water surging across Suffolk, as far inland as Snape.

The army had already arrived to help with the clean up operation and to help the local fishermen fill the huge gaps torn in the sea wall. Sadly, one fisherman drowned when his boat capsized in rough waters.

The Lovett home was near Jubilee Hall, used by the soldiers as a base camp and John's mother invited cold and exhausted servicemen in to enjoy a decent hot bath.

10 am - Great Wakering, Essex
Rescuers were still struggling against the gale force winds and severe tidal current. One elderly man rowing a boat struggled so hard against the water to get to the huts to help rescue people, that he ruptured himself and died. A female rescuer came across a toddler girl clinging to the roof of one of the huts, calling for her mummy. On the same roof was a man and a little boy, but no lady; she had passed out from the cold during the night and slipped off the roof to her death. The boy was also dead. The body of the 3 year-old boy, who had been sat on the floating table by his mother in a bid to get to safety, was also discovered.

10 am - Canvey Island, Essex
The water level in the Manser family's bungalow had begun to drop from the top of the window frames and more light was coming in. Suddenly they heard a noise; it was a boat that had come to rescue them from their terrible nightmare. Two men could be seen trying to slide open the veranda doors, but the water had made the wood swell and they were jammed shut. They told the family to stand clear and used their boat as a battering ram to smash the glass. Mrs Manser was taken away first and she held the bodies of her baby boys, Alan and Gordon, as they were rowed away. Fifteen minutes later Chris was taken, still clutching little Keith's body. The boat came again for Malcolm, Graham and Margaret, then finally Mr Manser and Andrew.

They were rowed to a house on the other side of the sea wall and passed up from the boat. The boys stood naked, except for vests, shivering and embarrassed that everyone could see them. Grown ups surrounded the children and dried and dressed them. The family waited on the wall with many other people to await instructions, the narrow concrete path ahead was flooded on both sides, but this seemed to be the only way off the island. Andrew Manser gazed around and looked southwards, down the roads on the other side of the wall. An old lady in a bungalow was refusing to leave her home and the rescuers had no choice but to leave her; she was to pay the price when the tide came back in, as she became another victim.

In a bungalow at Sunken Marsh, a couple in their early 70s had spent the last nine and a half terrifying hours standing on a dressing table, thigh deep in the water. The cries of people outside and splashing of water where people had fallen to their death had haunted them in the darkness of night. Now daylight had come, accompanied by an unbearable silence. Suddenly a noise shook them from their weakened daze; it was rescuers in a boat. The elderly couple were carried to the boat and rowed out of the marsh. They had no dentures or glasses and their nightclothes were soaked; they seemed oblivious to this as they looked around them and tried to take in the surrounding scene. The roads they knew so well were 6 feet underwater in places. One of the rescuers came out of their neighbour's bungalow shaking his head, they realised that they hadn't made it through the night. The couple were taken to Small Gains Creek wall where army lorries waited to take survivors. The lorries were full of half naked men, women, and children, nearly all sobbing and devastated.

The rescue operation was being hampered by a lack of information and a lack of boats. Reg Stevens, the island surveyor was still hard at work, doing his best to help save lives as the clock ticked and the tide was due back in. He asked a soldier to drive him in a lorry to a nearby industrial estate where there was a boat-making factory. They broke in and took as many boats as they could and headed back to the Admiral Jellicoe public house. News then came in that 120 boats were on their way from Southend. This couldn't have come at a more opportune time, the tide was rising again and was beginning to froth over the breached walls at Tewkes Creek again, putting the rescuers and flood survivors who were still trapped, in grave danger.

As the water level began to rise across the island, soldiers and volunteers battled against the waves in their boats as the winds blew up again. In the end the rescuers found it easier to jump out of the boats, into the chest deep water, and steered the boats from behind by pushing them against the will of the wind and water.

12 pm - Southend-on-Sea, Essex

The RSPCA man arrived back at his office and changed out of his wet uniform. He then telephoned the Chief Secretary for the RSPCA to see if he could round up some help to deal with the animal crisis on Canvey Island. The secretary immediately contacts some local veterinaries to lend their services and tells the officer to contact his own staff on an emergency basis.

1 pm - Canvey Island, Essex

Over at Sunken Marsh, a Scottish welder, who was working on a contract in the area and staying at the Admiral Jellicoe public house, had joined Kars Prium some hours previously. Both men had been working flat out rescuing the survivors of the flood and were now rowing around the outskirts of Sunken Marsh, when they heard a baby crying. The men rowed towards the sound and found the 8 week-old baby girl who had been tucked into her Moses basket for safety by her parents when the floodwaters came. The men did a brief search for the baby's parents, but couldn't see anything under the murky water just feet away from them. The men then set off hurriedly to the houseboat, so that the baby could be taken care of as soon as possible.

The Chief Medical Officers on the island had been taking water samples for testing and discovered, as feared, that raw sewage was now contaminating the floodwater. The army ordered that an immediate evacuation was compulsory and anyone refusing to leave the island would be removed by force.

2.30 pm - Netherlands

It had become clear that south western Holland had been lashed by the same storm that had caused Great Britain such devastation. 1,836 people had drowned when the dyke system couldn't cope with the mass of water and collapsed sending floodwater hurtling inland. The death toll, damage to arable land and loss of livestock was colossal compared to the U.K.

3 pm - Canvey Island, Essex

The man who had been helping Kars Prium, walked back into the Admiral Jellicoe and promptly collapsed with exhaustion. He was helped to a chair by his colleagues and given hot soup by the landlady as he recovered enough to tell them of the brave Dutchman and the terrible things he saw over at Sunken Marsh.

Denham Road. Rowing from Jones' Corner © Geoff Barsby

A police sergeant and a constable arrive at the refuge house over near Winter Gardens, where the Benfleet Yacht Club members had been taking the flood survivors. He congratulated the men and women on their selfless achievements, but came with a stern warning that the inner wall was in severe danger of collapsing. The house had to be evacuated at once. The sergeant sent for 6 ambulances to be sent to Central Wall to pick up the survivors.

As dusk fell across Canvey Island, so the concentrated burst of evacuation began to slow up. This gave some of the rescuers their first chance since the early hours to sit and rest, while firemen and volunteers from all over Essex descended on the island to lend a hand. A group of fireman from Ilford had discovered that Central Wall had now breached and they had begun rowing down New Road towards Winter Gardens. The whole area was now under water and the firemen began the mission of evacuation.

The atmosphere over at Sunken Marsh was eerie, the tide was very high again and had bubbled and belched its way back through the broken and half repaired sea walls, swallowing the island back up. The rescuers rowed down the flooded, silent streets, calling out to any survivors that were still trapped in their homes. The gas streetlamps were alight beneath the surface of the water and gave a ghostly glow as the boats passed silently above them. Only the creak of windows that had been left open and gentle knocking caused by floating debris was audible. Something between 200-600 people were feared to have lost their lives on the island and most of the bodies still lay where they had fallen. The rescuers felt the hairs on the backs of their necks prickle, as the thought of dead eyes watching, just out of sight, gave them the creeps. Men in boats looked for survivors, with the collars of their coats standing up and pulled tight around their necks as they tried to concentrate on the matter in hand.

Larup Avenue, Canvey Island

4.40 pm - Wallasea Island, Essex

Ten people had now been rescued from the island. Police had found the body of Charles Rolfe, who had accompanied the landlady as she tried to retrieve her coat, in the entrance to the Creeksea Ferry Inn. Rescuers had gone to Allfleets to try and find a postman, James Burns, who had last been seen leaving the Wallasea Bay Café on his pushbike. Inside his bungalow, the ceilings were smothered in grass and seaweed, but no sign of the postman.

Elsewhere along the east coast of Britain, the tide was flooding back in to the already crippled towns and villages. The streets of Mablethorpe in Lincolnshire were disappearing back under the sea, as she crept back in to mock the shattered residents and to boastfully claim what she had taken from them.

8 pm - Southtown, Great Yarmouth, Norfolk

Men in a boat finally rescue the signalman, stranded in his box near Southtown Railway Station, from his ordeal.

Scharendijk, Schouwen, Netherlands

Monday, 2nd February, 1953

<u>6 am - Foulness Island, Essex</u>
The officer in charge of operations on Foulness had received instructions to make a detailed reconnaissance. He only had a short amount of time to carry it out and this was at low tide. He set out in a DUKW and began at Fisherman's Head, leaving behind a rescue force and two warrant officers, so they could begin evacuating the residents. At Churchend the water was 3 feet in depth and as he passed through the little village some people in a house hailed him. He explained that he was on a mission and that rescuers were on their way.

Two elderly gentlemen being rescued from Foulness Island

As he approached Shelford he spotted a group of uniformed men; they were War Department constables and had been caught out by the sudden flood and stranded on top of their vehicle. The officer told them to jump aboard the DUKW and he would take them to a safer place. The men told him that they had been on their way to pick up another constable when the flood came; he was at Taylor's Hut over on Havengore Island. The water here was

6 feet deep and the officer was forced to turn the DUKW back on to Foulness. Hidden fences and other obstacles, making navigation almost impossible, blocked the path. The officer resorted to standing on the front of the vehicle with a long pole to feel his way through the deep, murky saltwater. It felt strange to the men as they passed trees full of rabbits and hedgerows littered with chickens.

On the return journey they stopped at Churchend and the officer took six villagers in the DUKW. Boats had already begun arriving from nearby Burnham-on-Crouch and were in the process of helping with the evacuation.

6.05 am - Canvey Island, Essex

The low tide allowed the repairmen to fix the broken telephone lines so that the island once again had communication to the mainland.

Larup Avenue

The men that had come to Canvey in their 'little ships' from Leigh-on-Sea, like those that assisted during the evacuation at Dunkirk, were out of action at low tide, so the men assisted with checking properties for any survivors. They trudged down the muddy streets in their wading boots, breaking the silence as they called out. The bungalows sat silently in the salty puddles. Their doors, with huge 'S' marks chalked on them to indicate they had already been searched, stood half-open leading into darkened hallways. Every garden was littered with vast amounts of white spaghetti knotted string, which on closer inspection proved to be dead worms, brought to the surface by the sea and bleached white by the salt. The fields were covered in them and as they dried out, the vile stench only added to the smell that was rising from the corpses of livestock and other animals.

Britain's east coast was in a state of shock; the sea had come in over the sea defences without warning. Hundreds of miles of coastline were smashed wide open and people's homes and lives had been torn apart. The worst was over and now began the task of picking up the pieces.

People abandoning Canvey, 1st February, 1953

Canvey, 3rd February

Chapter Eight

After the flood

In the days, weeks and months after that terrible night, more bodies were recovered and the death toll could finally be given. Some will argue that the number of fatalities was much higher due to the amount of deaths after the 1st February as a direct result of being submerged in ice-cold water for hours on end. Two people in Great Wakering who had been rescued from the Home Farm Camp, died of pneumonia and were not added to the official death toll and one dead body was found on Canvey Island some time after the official death toll was given. This was the case in nearly every town.

The body of the postman who had gone missing on Wallasea Island was found on 8th March in a 'delf ditch' on the other side of the sea wall. The occupiers of the farm on Havengore Island had last seen the missing War Department Constable Stanley Gray on the roof of Taylor's Hut. They said as night began to fall he must have decided that he didn't want to spend another freezing night up on the roof and he was seen trying to get back to Foulness through fairly deep water. His body was recovered on 29th March in the creek between New England Island and Havengore Island. The missing sister-in-law of the retired

Ambulance men rescue a man on Canvey

police officer, who had tried so hard to try and reach her little timber cottage and another female islander had both drowned. One body was discovered on 3rd February and the other on the 14th.

Canvey Island suffered the highest death toll; 58 people had lost their lives, eight of them under the age of 12. Many thought the island was going to have to be abandoned, but the hardy islanders returned with pride in their hearts and began to sweep the smelly silt and water out of their homes. The 600 missing islanders that had been presumed dead had barricaded themselves into their beloved homes and refused to budge! This dropped the estimated death toll for the island dramatically, but made all concerned realise what danger they were in. The sea walls needed to be rebuilt and raised way above the surge level to protect the island against future flooding. Some people admitted to setting their alarm clocks to wake them before a high tide was due in, so they wouldn't get caught out again.

The second highest death toll for the east coast was Felixstowe, where 39 people lost their lives, including the elderly couple at Point Clear Bay, and the third highest was Jaywick with 37 fatalities: 15 of the victims lived in Meadow Way and seven in Golf Green Road. These people were killed by the initial wave that had raced across the marshes from St Osyth. One of the victims was a female in the late stages of pregnancy. The tragedy was unbearable; it's no wonder many people moved away from the coast after the disaster.

Children caught up in the flood were either to be mentally scarred for life, unable to talk of their experiences, or simply saw the whole ordeal as a great adventure. The Manser family never returned to Canvey Island and moved into a house in one of the neighbouring towns. Mr and Mrs Manser never spoke of the tragedy for the rest of their lives, the remaining children never spoke about it among themselves for 50 years.

The baby found floating in the Moses basket was raised by her grandparents on Canvey Island; at 8 weeks old she would have no memory of that fateful night the sea snatched her parents from her.

Some of the flood tales are on a lighter note; Mrs Rosalind Boyce of Lincolnshire was a young girl in 1953, but lived further inland. Later that year, a school friend informed Rosalind how she and her family were going on holiday to Mablethorpe. Rosalind cast her mind back to when she heard the grown-ups discussing the floods and how there was 'only one house left in Mablethorpe'. This alarmed young Rosalind and she remembers being quite concerned that her friend would arrive in Mablethorpe and find only one house left!

Craven Avenue, Canvey Island

New sea wall near Shell Beach, Canvey Island. Remains of the old Dutch sea wall can be seen sticking out of the sand.

Chapter Nine

Flood Defences

The entire coastline from Lincolnshire along Norfolk, Suffolk, and Essex, down the length of the River Thames and around Kent had to be re-structured. The sea walls needed to be raised way above the 1953 surge level. Somewhere around 30,000 men set to work to repair the damaged sea defences, many of them British and US servicemen. The temperature was zero degrees Celsius, with sleet and snow showers driven by icy winds. Many breaches still remained unsealed by the 14th February, when the next unusually high tide was due in and the water continued to flood in at each full tide. Over a month later many areas still lay swamped in water until the populated areas had been protected. The 14th came and went otherwise uneventfully; as the tide came down the Thames, it turned earlier than predicted.

People frantically re-building the sea wall at Canvey against the next high tide

Londoners escaped flooding by the skin of their teeth. Millions were at risk in the densely populated capital. The London underground train system would have been filled as the Thames very nearly breached the embankments in the city. There was grave cause for concern over possible future flooding. Tower Hamlets, Hammersmith, and Wandsworth are just a few places sitting well below the 1953 surge level. A flood plan was needed immediately to avoid the danger that was literally breathing down London's neck. At first, Parliament discussed flooding old marshland along the Thames Estuary in Essex and Kent to lower the tide level. Unfortunately this included giving Canvey Island back to the sea and relocating the thousands of residents; this caused local uproar. This plan was soon quashed and a plan for a multi-million pound flood barrier to be erected in east London was much more favourable. Eventually after much research testing and arguing, London's new flood defence system began construction in 1976.

The Thames Barrier is the world's largest moving barrier and stretches the 520 meters across the River Thames at Woolwich in east London. Its design was picked from a possible 44 proposals entered and this particular design was favoured for its ability to keep the natural flow of the river and for the fact that shipping height wouldn't be restricted. The design was also picked, basically because it looked fantastic! The 6 gates are 5 storeys in height and 61 meters across. Each gate has its own hydraulic power system, housed below steel roofs. When the semi-circular gates open, they are positioned to lie flush against the riverbed, so there are no obstructions.

The barrier was finally opened in 1982 and has been raised about 64 times to 2003, as a flood precaution, but is raised monthly at low tide as a test drill.

One of the many flood gates on Canvey's sea wall (Thames front). These are open for the public to gain access to the beach and lower footpath. All but a few are permanently closed during the autumn/winter months.

Between 1974 and 1983 the flood defence system along the River Thames, from London and along the North bank towards Shoeburyness, was vastly improved. The total cost was somewhere in the region of £40 million, but the need to protect the low laying towns of south Essex and prevent a disaster in the capital were paramount. The riverbank between Purfleet and St Clements was strengthened with a concrete wall containing a short steel pile cut-off. At Grays Beach, near Grays town, a deep steel sheet piling wall encased in concrete was erected and given a decorative finish, to soften its appearance. This also provided a high level footpath for access to Grays Beach and the local yacht club. The flood defences at Tilbury's 17th century Coalhouse Fort had to be carefully thought through, so as not to interfere with the historic site. A deep steel sheet pile defence was erected on the foreshore and has to be restrained by anchors in a few places. A high level footpath was provided for visitors to the fort so that views across to Gravesend in Kent were uninterrupted. At East Tilbury the existing earth bank was reinforced with a new concrete crest wall with easy access to either side of the wall maintained.

Canvey Island needed many different types of sea defence for different areas of the island. The north of the island took the brunt of the 1953 flood and so needed more protection. This came in the form of a new concrete and steel pile wall filled with gravel at Sunken Marsh and a refuse wall reinforced with concrete blocks at Newlands. At Smallgains, the creek was dammed off and the ditches were piped; these are controlled by one of the islands many pumping stations. The bank at Eastern Esplanade that runs along the southern edge of the island was built by encasing long steel piles in concrete, widening the earthen bank on the roadside and the footpath on the beach side. This wall runs eastwards to Thorney Bay and out to the west to the Lobster Smack public house and Holehaven Creek. The Lobster Smack wall has steel sheet pile-clad in concrete and the old sea wall remains at Holehaven, but is backed up with a new earthen wall with a high concrete wall on top. A new ramp was built over the wall at Holehaven Causeway and at other areas on the eastern side of the island to provide causeway for boats to be transferred from land to sea.

Although great improvement has been made along the coastline, (including the operation to improve the defences in Leigh-on-Sea's old town, where the cobbles that make up the High Street had to be numbered when removed so that they could be replaced in the correct positions) the seafront coastline is still at risk from flooding. On numerous occasions over the years, the esplanade at Westcliff-on-Sea and Chalkwell has had to be closed to through traffic due to water spilling onto the road. A high tide will sometimes coincide with stormy weather, which results in large waves easily breaching the low esplanade wall and railings. The Environment Agency is currently working on a solution to this problem.

The Thames Barrier at Woolwich may be the most spectacular, but is not the only flood barrier along the River Thames. The Mardyke Sluice, a vertical floodgate, was installed to the west of Purfleet in Essex, stretching 5 and a half meters across the Mardyke and to a depth of just over 2 and a half meters. The Tilbury Dock floodgate was installed to protect the busy docks and is 33 and a half meters wide and sits at a depth of 18 meters. It is kept in a horizontal position and is rolled across the lock during exceptionally high tides. A dam was constructed across Mucking Creek to protect the heavily populated town of Stanford-le-Hope. The dam has 2 openings, which are 1 and a half meters square. Three barriers were built in the waters surrounding Canvey Island; one at Fobbing Horse (a small uninhabitable island in Vange Creek between Canvey Island and Fobbing), one in Easthaven Creek and one in Benfleet Creek. Fobbing Horse Barrier has a huge gate measuring over 36 meters across and over 9 meters deep. The gate sits 9 meters above spring tide level to allow traffic through until it is needed to be lowered. The Easthaven Barrier has 3 separate openings that are also held above spring tide level, but only 3 meters above. The gates are nearly 9 meters deep. The central opening is 12 meters across and is for river traffic to pass through. The other two openings serve the natural flow of the water. The Benfleet Barrier can be seen closely if you pass over the bridge on to the island near Benfleet Rail station. This barrier also has 3 openings, each measuring 12 meters across. The central 'navigation gate' is 6 meters deep and the 2 'tidal gates' are 5 and a half meters deep, all 3 sit horizontally, 2 meters above the flow of the creek until the need to lower them arises.

The Environment Agency not only monitor the tides at these points, but from the Humber Estuary down the entire coastline, into all the creeks and rivers along the way and into the Thames. The coastal monitoring consists of 5 components; beach surveys, surveys of the seabed, aerial photography, inspections of sea defences and beaches and the levels of water, wind and waves. The NRA (National Rivers Association) are also responsible for monitoring river levels and conditions of riverbanks and defences. Water levels are also obtained from the Proudman Oceanographic Laboratory and information on wind and waves is taken from the Meteorological Office.

Blue Circle Cement Company, West Thurrock.
Picture by Valerie Stone, who was a secretary working in the offices.

Future flood defences are always being considered due to the ever-rising tidal levels. Trials for a new type of flood defence were in operation at Cabborns Marsh near Stanford-le-Hope, but due to the poor waterlogged and silty material that was present to an enormous depth, the trial failed. This happened a number of times with different designs. New experiments are currently underway with alternative bank raising methods being tested. These have proved to be more successful, but at a cost of £104 million (the total cost for the East Anglia region's Tidal Defence works).

Floodgates near Stanford le Hope

The Environment Agency also run a successful Flood Warning system for the U.K. Information is gathered from their own resources and compared with reports from the Met. Office and the Storm Tide Forecasting Service. Warnings are then issued to the emergency services, the public and local authorities. There are four warning levels; Flood Watch, Flood Warning, Severe Flood Warning and All Clear. Flood Watch warns of possible flooding 'Be aware! Be Prepared! Watch Out!' Flood Warning warns of flooding expected 'affecting many homes, businesses and main roads. Act now!' The Severe Flood Warning warns of severe flooding expected, 'Imminent danger to life and property. Act now!' Then finally the All Clear tells of 'No Flood Watches or Warnings in force. Water levels receding. Check all is safe to return. Seek advice.'

The government and the Environment Agency are constantly considering new ways to protect our coastal and riverside towns and villages. New walls and barriers will be built in the future, but it won't be long until we have to finally succumb to the constant rising sea levels and eventually end up giving land back to the sea in order to save ourselves. One successful experiment where land was given back took place in Salcott Creek, just off the River Blackwater in Essex. Hundreds of acres of land were successfully flooded, thus helping to lower the tide further downstream and giving villagers living along the river, peace of mind during high tides. Local oyster fishermen were concerned that the riverbed would become contaminated during the experiment and kill the oysters; this would have spelt disaster for the men's livelihood. The project was so successful, actually nourishing the oyster beds, that now the oystermen are willing to back more experiments of this nature, along the river.

Jaywick's sea front after the Storm. © *Essex Police Museum*

Chapter Ten

Memorials and the 50th Anniversary commemorations

Several towns have erected flood plaques of memorials to remember those who died or acted with extraordinary bravery on the night of the flood. Canvey Island has a bronze plaque on the library wall in the town centre. It lists the names and ages of the 58 people who lost their lives. For the 50th anniversary a new flood memorial has been created and is situated on Canvey seafront, on the Labworth recreational ground.

The Paddocks community hall held a Civic Commemoration Service for the 50th anniversary in which 350 people attended. The Mayor of Castle Point, Charles Smith, and Councillor Ray Howard were in attendance and after the ceremony they lit a new beacon, which has been erected on the roundabout at Waterside Farm. This beacon will be lit on every 31st January and 1st February for years to come in memory of the dead.

The townspeople of Sutton-on-Sea held a very successful reunion dinner and many braved the icy conditions to attend. Prince Phillip unveiled a plaque at the Dunes Family

Entertainment Centre in Mablethorpe to commemorate the anniversary of the floods and a new memorial was erected in Snettisham, made of a brick pillar with a bright blue plaque with yellow writing. It has a picture of the setting sun and the words IN MEMORY OF THOSE WHO LOST THEIR LIVES IN THE FLOODS AT SNETTISHAM IN 1953.

Many towns held exhibitions to show photos of the flood and to reunite flood victims to tell their stories, sad tales, and amusing memories.

The people of Norway donated 20 houses to Rochford District Council for the people who lost their homes in areas such as Great Wakering. The timber cast houses were built in

Norway and shipped to the Baltic Wharf on Wallasea Island. From there they were transported to Ashingdon, where they still stand at Nansen Avenue and Ashingdon Road.

In Stranraer's Agnew Park, a memorial to the victims of the *Princess Victoria* ferry disaster was unveiled in 1962. The plaque mounted on a mound of boulders with a heavy anchor, reads;

"On the morning of 31ˢᵗ January 1953, the M V Princess Victoria *left the east pier, Stranraer, to make its normal crossing to Larne. Off Corsewall Point, the ship encountered the full fury of the gale which was to cause so much damage and loss of life throughout the country, and, despite the valiant efforts of her crew, the lifeboatmen and other seafarers, the* Princess Victoria *foundered off the coast of Northern Ireland with the loss of 133 lives. Of those lost, 23 were inhabitants of Stranraer, whose death this community mourns."*

On the 50ᵗʰ anniversary, there was a memorial service and another plaque was added to the Agnew Park memorial. This plaque lists the names of all the disaster victims. There was also a memorial service out at sea for the families of the victims. P & O ferries put on a special ferry to take the families out to where the *Princess Victoria* was last seen. Wreaths were cast out, hymns were sung, and prayers said in honour of the dead.

Canvey Island's new flood memorial in
1953 Garden of Remembrance.

RECOMMENDED READING

Barsby, Geoff: Canvey Island [Archive Photographs series]. Chalford
Barsby, Geoff: Canvey Island, the second selection. Chalford
Barsby, Geoff: 1953 remembered. Barsby
Brown, Paul: The Wivenhoe & Brightlingsea Railway. Ian Henry
Cameron, Stephen: Death in the North Channel
Currie, Ian, *and others*: The Essex weather book. Froglets
Grieve, Hilda: The Great Tide. Essex County Council
Harland, M G *and* H J: The flooding of Eastern England. Minimax
Hussey, Stephen: Essex headlines. Essex Record Office
McCave, Fred: History of Canvey Island. Ian Henry
Pollard, Michael: North Sea surge. Dalton
Smith, Ken: Canewdon: a pattern of life through the ages. Ian Henry
Summers, Dorothy: East coast floods. David & Charles
Yearsley, Ian: Islands of Essex. Ian Henry

A rescue on Beveland, Netherlands

REPORTED DEATHS FROM THE GREAT STORM

Michael Griffith fatalities

Charles Singleton
Leonard Grundy
J T Wilson
Harry Anderson
Thomas Burns
W Hargreave
R Bodden
J Tucker
S J Johns
J Cryson
C Murdoch
Georle Palin
A Bidle

Princess Victoria Official Death Toll (135 persons)

CREW
Robert Campbell Ball, Windsor Rd, Belfast - aged 25 (5th engineer)
Roseanne Baxter, Gardenmore Park, Larne - aged 39 (stewardess)
William C Blair, Glynnview Avenue, Larne - aged 33 (steward)
Charles Boreland, Belmont Road, Stranraer (chief steward)
Hugh Brennan, Crescent Gardens, Larne - aged 45 (purser)
David Broadfoot, Royal Crescent, Stranraer - aged 53 . (wireless operator)
John A Campbell, Ailsa Crescent, Stranraer (able seaman)
Catherine Clarke, Arran Road, Gourock, Renfrew (bureau assistant)
Mary Close, Bay Park, Larne (bureau assistant)
Shirley Duckels, Bowling Green Road, Stranraer (Chief Officer)
James Millar Ferguson, Craigenelder, Stranraer (Captain)
Edmond Freel, Ashbrook Crescent, Belfast - aged 29 (4th engineer)
William Gowan, Glencairn House, Portavogie - aged 26 (ship's carpenter)
William Hardy, Broomfield Gardens, Stranraer (quartermaster)
William Hooper, Bank Road, Larne - aged 17 (pantry boy)
Wesley Kerr, Fleet Street, Larne - aged 25 (steward)
Fergie Leckie, Sun Street, Stranraer (quartermaster)
Horace Locke, Albert Street, Larne (pantry man)
Alexander McAllister, John Simpson Drive, Stranraer (greaser)

William McCarlie, Dalrymole Street, Stranraer (bosun)
James McCowan, McDowall Drive, Stranraer - aged 50 (2nd steward)
William McGarel, Glynn Road, Larne - aged 55 (quartermaster)
William McInnes, Fairhurst Avenue, Stranraer - (2nd engineer)
David McMillan, John Simpson Drive, Stranraer - aged 21 (pantry man)
William Mann, Coastguard Road, Larne - aged 59 (luggage man)
James Mayne, Curran Street, Larne (assistant steward)
Gerald Morgan, Beechwood Avenue, Stranraer - aged 33 (steward)
James A Morrow, Carnalbana, Ballymena - aged 33 (assistant purser)
Douglas Murray, Glynn Road, Larne - aged 43 (greaser)
Archibald O'Neill, Glynnview Avenue, Larne - aged 27 (steward)
William Parker, Waterloo Road, Larne - aged 35 (2nd Steward)
John Peoples, Recreation Road, Larne - aged 16 (mess room steward)
John Porter, Royal Avenue, Stranraer (3rd engineer)
Edward Pritchard, Mountvemon Road, Stranraer (assistant cook)
James Rankin, Murrayfield Gardens, Stranraer (greaser)
Allan Ross, Church Street, Stranraer (2nd steward)
Patrick Shields, Roddens Terrace, Larne - aged 28 (assistant steward)
John Taylor, Regent Park Grove, Morecambe, Lancashire - (2nd engineer)
Albert Thomas, Fairhurst Avenue, Stranraer (chief engineer)
John Wallace, Agnew Crescent, Stranraer - aged 24 (night steward)
Leonard White, West Point, Ballygally (2nd officer)
John A. Wilton, Enfield Street, Portstewart - aged 23

PASSENGERS
Northern Ireland

Belfast

Samuel Harris Brown, Antrim Rd
James Curry, Roden Street
Thomas Gault, Martinez Avenue - aged 43
William Hammond, Little Victoria Street - aged 23
Annie Jackson MBE, Eglantine Street
Major Frank Jewhurst (53d AA Workshop Co. REME), Cherryhill Drive, Dundonald - aged 60
Florence Johnstone, Rushfield Avenue

Robert Kelly, Wallasey Park
James Lowe BEM, Flush Green - aged 50
Thomas J Lowther, Thorburn Rd
Dominic McCarter, Walmer Street
Mr McClatchy
William McCleneghan, Mealough, Carryduff - aged 28
James McKay, North Approach Road
Mr R McLaughlin, Cullintree Road
Agnes McNeill, Ava Drive (pregnant)
Ronald McNeill, Ava Drive
Helen Magill - aged 35
John Magill
Victor Mitchell, Espie Way - aged 30
Hubert Moore, Richardson Street - aged 48
Martha Moore, Richardson Street
Victor Moore, Richardson Street - aged 8
Thomas Moreton, Ainsworth Avenue
William Nassau Parker, Ava Gardens
John Spence Piggot, Osbourne Gardens - aged 28
Lennox Donald Piggot, Osbourne Gardens - aged 19
Adam M Reid, Armitage Street
Ivan Campbell Robinson, Neely Street - aged 27
Robert J Rosborough, Ogilvie Street - aged 36
J. Maynard Sinclair MP (Stormont), Deramore Park South - aged 57
Robert White, Sterling Avenue - aged 33
Norman Willis, Severn Street

Co Antrim

Thompson Bonnar, Mill Street, Larne - aged 48
William Carter, Camcastle, Larne - aged 35
Thomas Clarke, Owenstown, Ballysnod, Larne - aged 19
Harry Coleman, Drains Bay, Larne - aged 38
Robert Craig, Upper Waterloo Road - aged 49
Elizabeth Crawford, Galgorm Street, Ballymena - aged 48
William Dummigan, Newington Avenue, Larne - aged 65
David W Hamilton, Gortin, Camlough - aged 22
Jane Hanna, Troopers Lane, Carrickfergus
Adam Heggarty, Gloucester Avenue, Larne - aged 23
Alexander McCready, Ballylumford, Island Magee - aged 61
Andrew McMurty, Drummond Street, Larne - aged 56
Margaret Magee, Drumraymond, Toomebridge - aged 20
Iris Mooney, Knockatyde View, Ballycastle
John Noble Mooney, Ballycastle - aged 5
Kevin Mooney, Ballycastle - aged 2
James Morrow, Roddens Lane, Larne
Wolsey W Patterson, West Street, Carrickfergus
Ada Prior, The Bay, Camlough

Samuel M Reynolds, Rosebrook, Carrickfergus - aged 37
Robert Ritchie, Newington Avenue, Larne - aged 22

Co Derry

Nancy Adair Bryson, Cremona, Castlerock - aged 44
David Francey, Moneymore - aged 20
Dudley Farnsworth Kipling, Limavady Road, Derry - aged 65
Mary Gunn, Draperstown (3 mths pregnant)
Isabella Milligan, Tobermore Road, Magherafelt - aged 64
Sgt. Francis Mullan (Irish Fusiliers), Ballymully, Limavady - aged 29
Rose Mary Mullan, Coolnasillagh, Garvagh - aged 22
Geraldine Wordsworth, Maghera

Co Down

Robert McNair Connolly, Mary Street, Newtownards - aged 36
Alfred McCready, Greyabbey Road, Ballywalter
Lieut. Col. Sir Walter D. Smiles MP, Portavogie Point - aged 70

Co Armagh

Richard Mason, Markethill

Eire

Edwin Fitzgerald, Oliver Plunkett Avenue, Dun Laoghaire, Co Dublin - aged 32
Patrick J McLaughlin, Dungloe, Co Donegal - aged 29
Lily Russell, Kiltoy, Letterkenny, Co Donegal - aged 27
Sgt. James Sumner (Royal Inniskilling Fusilers), Clownel, Co Tipperary
Mr Sweeny, Dublin

Scotland

William Ferguson Borland, Belmont Road, Stranraer
Eileen Carlin, St Ninian Place, Prestwick, Ayrshire - aged 33
Marie Connery, Carrick Drive North, Glasgow - aged 40
Mary Connery, Carrick Drive North, Glasgow
Catherine Driver, Earlstone Avenue, Glasgow - aged 32
Ian McDonald, Broomfield Gardens, Stranraer - aged 28
Phillomena McDowell, Whitsun Avenue, Stranraer - aged 19
Flight Sgt. Alex Petrie (RAF), Loch Ryan Street, Stranraer - aged 28

England

Lieut. Comm. A N Bilney (RN), RAF Anthorn, Cumberland
Rebecca Hayes Thompson Bilney, RAF Anthorn, Cumberland
Joyce Childs, Green Road, Southsea, Hampshire - aged 24
Leslie Childs, Green Road, Southsea, Hampshire
Stephen Childs, Southsea, Hampshire - aged 3
George H Clarke, Cooperative Street, Derby
WRNS Violet Dingle, Enfield, London - aged 19
David Gillanders, Benton, Northumberland - aged 26
Rebecca Hayes, Bilney, Norfolk
Joseph O'Connor, Gateshead, Northumberland - aged 65
Eileen Prentice, Downe, Farnborough, Hampshire
Mr A P Rowlands, Durranhill, Carlisle, Cumberland - aged 21
C.P.O. Gerald Shankland (RN), Hilltop Avenue, Chester
Flight Sgt. Albert Tatchel (RAF), Corfelcastle, Devon - aged 50

ESSEX

CANVEY ISLAND
Adelsberg Road
    Margaret Blagdon
    Dennis Morgan, aged 5
    Phoebe Morgan, aged 72
    Reginald Morgan, aged 37
Amid Road
    Alice Lloyd, aged 79
Athos Road
    John Laverack, aged 60 (visitor from Edmonton)
Brandenberg Road
    Alice Brooks, aged 81
    Daisy Deith, aged 68
    Ernest Deith, aged 70
Church Parade
    Elizabeth Jacobs, aged 67
    James Jacobs, aged 68
    Emily Price, aged 88
Corona Road
    Emily Carter, aged 75
    Louisa Le May, aged 63
Craven Avenue
    Marie White, aged 65
Denham Road
    Catherine Rawkins, aged 87
Deventer Road
    Rebecca Keymer, aged 74
Gills Avenue
    Rose Hindle, aged 68

Heeswick Road
    Harriet Coates
    William Coates, aged 56
    Alice Farrow, aged 58
Heilsberg Road
    Alfred Hagen, aged 60
    Mary Hagen, aged 60
Juliers Road
    Matilda Tearle, aged 66
Kamerwyck Avenue
    Nora Dearman, aged 63
Kellington Road
    Doris Fairs, aged 46
    Elsie Foster, aged 26
    Ernest Foster, aged 32
Knightswick Road
    Katherine Fuller, aged 66
    Walter Fuller, aged 68
Komberg Crescent
    Julia Goodman, aged 4
Lansberg Road
    Hannagh O'Donohue, aged 60
Larup Avenue
    Julia Rennison, aged 76
May Avenue
    Ian Nelson, aged 7
Miltzin Avenue
    Arthur Hobbs, aged 65
    Agnes Simkins, aged 57
    Caroline Smitges, aged 69
Newlands Road
    Alice Smith, aged 74
    Edith White, aged 60
    William White, aged 62
Nordland Road
    Caroline Welham, aged 67
Park Road
    Alice B Lloyd, aged 70
Rainbow Road
    Gertrude Whines, aged 68
Somnes Avenue
    Alan Manser, aged 1
    Gordon Manser, aged 2
    Keith Manser, aged 5
Stanley Road
    Charlotte Flight, aged 72
    Henson Flight, aged 76
Strasbourg Road
    Peter Weston, aged 5
The Avenue
    Arthur Fisher, aged 62
Vadsoe Road
    Alice Davidson, aged 63
Waalwyck Drive
    Edward Curtis, aged 83
    Harriet Curtis, aged 83

Whernside Avenue
Leonard Starling, aged 12
Violet Starling, aged 36
Gertrude Williams, aged 65

FOULNESS ISLAND
Captain F A Cook, King's Head, aged 60
War Dept. Policeman Stanley Gray, Sutton Road,
Rochford (on duty Havengore Island)
Bertha Rawlings, Crouch Cottages, Courtsend, age 64
Violet Rawlings, Fisherman's Head, aged 41

GREAT WAKERING
Home Farm Camp
Stuart Curtis, aged 3
Ellen Kirby, aged 69
George Kirby, aged 71
David Whitehead, aged 4
Nellie Whitehead, aged 24
Landwick Cottages
William Driscoll, aged 40
New Road
Walter Manning, aged 67

HARWICH
Albert Street
Gladys Bruce, aged 23
Pauline Bruce, aged 16 months
Mr Mallows
Anchor Hotel
Pearl Lofts
Fernlea Road
Edward Ellis, aged 68
Grafton Road
Mr Vincent
Station Road
Frederick Shipley
Lilian Shipley

JAYWICK
Beach Crescent
Jessie French, aged 77
Cornflower Road
Ada Kendall, aged 62
Maria Miles, aged 42
Lucy Wilson, aged 73
Samuel Wilson, aged 71

Flowers Way
Dorothy Hamilton-Ross, aged 71
Glebe Way
Florence Brookman, aged 66
Hilda Brookman, aged 37
Golf Green Road
Edward Bishop, aged 80
Florence Bishop

Florence Buckle, aged 67
Harry Buckle, aged 70
Miss Laycock, aged 78
Ernest Rogers, aged 65
Rose Saward, aged 45
Meadow Way
Helena Bangle, aged 62
Nellie Burnett, aged 69
Sarah Dempster (visitor from Wood Green),
aged 61
Harriet Fox, aged 74
Esther Jew, aged 89
James Jew, aged 86
James Jew (visitor from Wood Green), aged
60
James Ketley, aged 74
May Ketley, aged 68
Lavinia Lambert, aged 71
Herbert Law, aged 76
Margarita Law, aged 74
Maude Pym, aged 69
Emma Scott, aged 78
Florence Weatherburn, aged 69
Singer Avenue
Joseph Bryson, aged 38
Lilian Bryson, aged 41
Michael Dervil, aged 11
Triumph Avenue
Anne Payne, aged 69
Reginald Payne, aged 38

POINT CLEAR
Mr & Mrs W J Crosswell, Point Clear Stores

SOUTHEND ON SEA
Henry James Ashwood, Burnaby Road
William Glover, Victoria Road, aged 65

WALLASEA ISLAND
James Burns, The Bungalow, Grass Farm Cottages,
aged 70
Charles Rolfe (visitor from Rochford), aged 43

KENT
BELVEDERE
George Ross, aged 81 [nightwatchman of Fredk.
Boehm, Ltd., Crabtree Manor Way and Belvedere
Sluice]

SUFFOLK

FELIXSTOWE
Langer Road
Brenda Bushnall, aged 6 months
Jean Bushnall, aged 26
Keith Bushnall, aged 2

INDEX

In the above index
C = Canvey Island
GW = Great Wakering
GY = Great Yarmouth
H = Harwich
KL = King's Lynn
L = Leigh on Sea
PH = Public House